4 HOUR YOUTH MINISTRY
ESCAPING THE TRAP OF FULL-TIME YOUTH MINISTRY

TIMOTHY ELDRED
AUTHOR OF PRAY21

4-HOUR YOUTH MINISTRY

ESCAPING THE TRAP OF FULL-TIME YOUTH MINISTRY

© 2010 Timothy Eldred

International Standard Book Number: 978-0-9796551-2-8

Unless otherwise indicated, Scripture quotations are from:

The Message by Eugene Petersen. © 1993, 1994, 1995, 1996, 2000, 2001, 2002.
Used by permission of NavPress Publishing Group.

Other Scripture quotations are from:

The Holy Bible, New International Version® (NIV).
© 1973, 1978, 1984 by International Bible Society.
Used by permission of Zondervan Publishing House.
All rights reserved.

Holy Bible, New Living Translation (NLT), second edition.
© 2004 by Tyndale House Publishers, Inc. All rights reserved.

ALL RIGHTS RESERVED.

No part of this publication may be reproduced, stored in a retrieval system, or transmitted, in any form or by any means—electronic, mechanical, photocopying, recording, or otherwise—without prior written permission.

Published by:

Christian Endeavor International
PO Box 377, 424 East Main Street
Edmore, MI 48829 USA
800.260.3234
christianendeavor.com

To Cindy

Twenty years of listening to me, as I listened for God's voice.

Twenty years of believing he was leading, as I followed.

Twenty years I wouldn't change and can never begin to repay.

I love you.

TABLE OF CONTENTS

Preface 5

Introduction: Quit Your Job 14

Chapter One: Defining Success 31

Chapter Two: Redefining Success 51

Chapter Three: Restructuring Time 70

Chapter Four: Understanding the B-Pyramid™ 90

Chapter Five: Recommitment to Youth 127

Chapter Six: Reconfiguring Your Role 150

Conclusion: 175

Appendix: Christian Endeavor Model 181

PREFACE

An ounce of prevention is worth a pound of cure.

I have never really thought much about that saying before sitting down to write this book, but it has really become what 4-Hour Youth Ministry is about.

Prevention.

As I have turned 40, that word has more meaning. This is the age when you start paying attention to what your doctor says. There are new tests and examinations. You begin to feel your age. Even this week, I have made daily exercise a priority again.

Or at least I'm trying.

It is funny how certain seasons of life get your attention. You wonder how things might have been different. For instance, would I feel better if I had worked harder at my health at 30?

Probably.

And it wouldn't have required triathlon training either. A few hours a week at the most doing the right things would have produced a better result. Eat less. Move more. Easy. Common sense.

So why do we ignore the obvious?

I can only answer that question for me, but I won't be surprised if you share my sentiments. I think we're too busy. Too busy caring.

Caring about the wrong things.

For twenty years, I have spent my life in youth ministry. Not a wrong thing for sure. We're all called to discover our ministry. But maybe in the midst of our mission we get focused or fixated on the wrong stuff. By accident. Unimportant stuff. As a result, the obvious becomes the obscure. Even neglected.

Exercise. Diet. Rest.

Ignored.

While I was busy trying to build a ministry and a reputation, I wasn't paying attention. I was too concerned with the wrong stuff about me to focus on the right stuff about others. Instead of trusting God for the increase, I was increasingly ignoring the way He works. Eventually, it became my ministry.

I found myself being more controlling. There have definitely been times when it was my way or the highway. And I even chose to call it leadership.

When you place yourself in control, everything is up to you. If it fails, it's your fault. Success. Same. The pressure is huge. Self-inflicted. Unnecessary. I suggest it stems from not paying attention.

Ignoring the obvious.

A few years ago, a friend and mentor challenged me with the idea that from cover-to-cover, the Bible was really about one word: stewardship. Think about it. God gave us creation, and He basically said, "Steward it." He gave us family, relationships, time, talent, treasure, and the Gospel.

Again, "Steward it."

As we consider our calling and ministry and recognize that God is control, stewardship makes more sense. He gave us a place to serve and platform from which to influence others. He leads us. We steward the opportunity.

I was sitting in my office a number of years ago, when a new friend called. God had placed him in my life at a very strategic time when I needed to learn some important lessons. He called to ask a simple question.

"What is your job?"

Now, at the time I had a title, job description, and ego to match. I shot back with a hasty answer. "I cast vision for a talented team of people and keep the focus of this ministry clear and our direction concise." Something ignorant like that.

"Wrong." Click.

He was gone. I think the silence on the other end was a clear indication that I failed the test. Now what? I determined to think harder, so the next time he called I'd have a real answer. I couple of days later, he phoned. I basically gave the same response in a different way. Wrong. Again.

Thankfully, this seasoned veteran, corporate CEO was patient enough with me to clue me in. "Your job is to release people's potential. Period." He continued, "Paul says it this way in Ephesians 4:12, 'Equip saints for the work of service…' That's your job. Help others be successful in their ministry."

As I mentioned earlier, we're all called to discover our mission in life. Some of us have accepted the responsibility to set others up for success. We have the honor of stewarding them, which simply means helping them become who God intended.

Of all the lessons I have learned, this one has been the hardest for me. It goes against my nature. It even flies in the face of culture. And that means today's church culture, too.

I am still working to understand the wisdom that has been shared with me. Even though I have taught these principles for many years now, I still fail often to follow them. Like you, I'm still learning.

This book isn't about another proven model of youth ministry that makes you jump through hoops or adapt someone else's accidental success. Like proper, balanced exercise, diet, and rest, 4-Hour Youth Ministry is a simple recipe for prevention.

Maybe you struggle like I do with listening. Oh, I hear people talk, but I don't always listen. If I was better at heeding the advise of others, I could have avoided some costly mistakes. When I say costly,

I'm referring to the mistakes that damaged and hurt others along the way. They paid a much higher price for my learning than me because I didn't choose to listen well.

When I was a teen my mom said, "If people don't like you for who are that's their problem, but right now you're being an idiot."

If I would have just chosen to listen better then. Even now. Life is about choices. Choices have consequences. Consequences produce chaos. I've created my share that could have been prevented.

And prevention is simply a choice.

This book is designed to help you prevent the pitfalls of a ministry that you run, you control, you own. The process is simple and puts God front and center and places you in your proper role as more of a steward and less of a leader.

It is really a book on ministry management. The primary elements deal with time, relationships, and trust. I'll present a process that challenges you to care about the right stuff and not ignore the obvious. You'll learn to understand what's really important and what's not. Most important, you'll be more efficient and learn to accomplish more by doing less more effectively.

After too many years of trial and error, I'm at a place I would never trade. I work less. Accomplish more. And see God change lives. Nothing could ever make me go back to full-time youth ministry. Or at least not the way it has been defined in the last few decades.

My love for Jesus and my love for teens just won't allow it. I hope this book changes your mind, too.

INTRODUCTION

QUIT YOUR JOB

So what is 4-Hour Youth Ministry? It's not a pipe dream. Not a fairytale. It's one big idea.

Breakthrough. Boiling all the work of ministry down to a few hours a week, so you can spend the rest of your time mentoring. Leading kids into a lifelong relationship with Jesus Christ. Period.

We're embarking on a journey using a new map. On

a different route than you're used to traveling. With directions simple enough that anyone, any church, any size, anywhere can follow.

I am going to show you how I learned to cut full-time youth ministry down to 4 hours and be more effective than ever. Seriously. The rest of my effort away from my first ministry, my family, was used to build enduring relationships. Ones that paid better dividends and produced a greater yield than all the time I spent running a youth program.

Paradigm shift for me. For sure.

Now, shift happens. But it doesn't occur without a clear plan of attack. Breaking patterns and behaviors can be tough. Real change requires discipline.

We're not just talking about changing your ministry model. This is a matter of altering your mind-set.

Determining to think differently in two key areas:

- Redefining youth ministry.
- Reconfiguring your role.

In a very real sense, you're going to learn how to quit your job. Fire yourself. And take on a new ministry description. As you work your way through the book, you'll see how God changed my thinking and learn to abandon tasks you've always done (and believed no one else could or should do) while picking up some new habits.

Better habits. Healthier.

The words of a young youth pastor in Canada might best describe the monster we're going to tackle.

"Tim, I didn't answer God's call to be a program director who plans meetings to make church leaders happy only to have little, if any, impact on kids."

Amen, sister. Me neither.

Does her apparent aggravation hit home for you? You're a full-time youth pastor who feels like you spend more hours managing programs than actually doing ministry. Maybe you're a pastor of a small congregation trying to encourage the efforts of volunteers who need some direction, but you don't feel like you have the right answers. Or maybe you are that volunteer who just bought the newest book or got home from a conference with all the answers. And you still don't know where to begin.

Regardless of your situation, I bet you feel our Canadian friend's frustration at some level. Because this is the rest of your story…

You love Jesus Christ! No doubt. In your life, he has revealed himself in such a complete way you can't help but share his message. Even more, you have a passion for reaching young people. You desperately want them to experience the transformed life only he can offer. There's no time to waste.

That's your real heartbeat. But this is your reality...

Day after day, week after week, year after year (even church after church), you prayerfully seek God's direction for a way to attract youth to a program you find yourself creating and a presentation of the gospel that appeals to kids. One that is pretty, polished, and of course, professional.

After hours of preparation, you watch, wait, and expect a crowd to come. Not only that, you believe your hard work will actually make a noticeable mark on their impressionable young lives.

When it doesn't generate spiritual growth, you look at new trends, steal ideas from other churches (even give them credit). You read the blogs, own the books, and book a trip to the next latest and greatest youth ministry convention.

Let's make it real. Most of your days are spent in an office at a desk, in a book, or behind a computer. Planning.

Am I close? Too close for comfort?

Now, let's say you're a volunteer youth leader and not in vocational youth ministry. Same deal. Just less time. Less money. More frustration. You have to get the same results with limited amounts of...everything. Only you're not going to get axed if you can't draw a bigger crowd than the church down the street.

Somehow, the job you signed up for and reality experienced a major disconnect. Out of nowhere, you've managed to become a program director (which is kind of like a wedding planner for kids working for minimum wage with wimpy health benefits and a bad vacation package).

Not what you thought it would be, huh? This isn't the job you signed up for.

Image this instead.

A group of young people look to you for guidance day after day, week after week, and year after year (without you moving from church after church). They have learned that you care deeply about their cause, their passion, their life. They have no doubt you're on their team, in their corner. They have learned to trust you with their ideas and dreams that you help become reality (not steal or make them your own). You set teens up for greater success. Instead of asking them to come to an event you invented, you invest in theirs. Help them achieve their goals.

You've got their back.

And they have your time.

As you speak with God in prayer, you simply ask for the ability to see beyond the surface of what others overlook in young lives. Those entrusted to your care. You seek strength to stay the course. Serve on their team. And release their unlimited potential.

It's not your job to do ministry for young people. You're a coach. A guide who helps them with their ministry. Not a program director. But a mentor.

Instead of sitting at a desk for hours pulling out your hair to come up with fresh ideas that fit your budget, you're taking inventory. Discerning how to leverage the talent on the team. The question on your mind everyday is how can I help Jennifer, Jeffrey, or little Junior become what God intended? And what position are they best suited to play?

As you remember your own spiritual development,

you recall people not programs that impacted you most. So you seek out adults with the personalities, skills, abilities, and time you lack. Mature followers of Jesus who might only have a few minutes a week to give, but desperately want to do something significant. They're just like the teens in that way (only older—with jobs and heavier beards).

In conversations over coffee, you teach them how simple it is to use their limited availability to unleash to ability of young people on the world in Jesus' name. It starts with a commitment. To pray.

Sure. They can do that.

It grows into healthy relationships. You model how. They catch the idea. Understand their role. They mentor. Teach youth how but never do it for them.

You find yourself making a real difference outside the office. Daily. While youth sit in school, you set the stage. Not for the worship band on Wednesday nights. For effective and consistent discipleship.

That's your job.

You're a mentor of mentors.

People in your church are beginning to see today's teens differently because you're sharing your heart, your passion, your belief in God's call on this generation with more and more of them. More consistently. And as people build relationships, they build bridges to a hurting generation.

Inter-generational ministry. That was easy.

And God changes them from the inside to see youth more differently than ever. They actually remember their own adolescence again. Empathy grows.

At the end of each day, you find yourself running out

of time to plan events, activities, and meetings.

Don't worry.

Those young people who you are getting to know and who are being cared for by a team of trained mentors are putting their faith in action. They are now the ones creating an atmosphere that attracts their peers. In an environment they prayerfully dream up and develop themselves.

Youth meetings are now based on their desires, their hurts, their heartaches for their world. Call it their program. Their ministry. Done by them. Taught how by others like you and those on your team.

Teens are digging into God's Word to better understand how it applies to their projects. And their lives. The bible is no longer a book with lists of don'ts. God is teaching them how to do instead. Their seeing their faith touch others.

In the past, you've schemed and screamed to get them to attend and appreciate all your efforts only to find more empty seats. More than will please many people in your church. But now they're coming. They're caring. It's their ministry. They're even bringing friends.

You have moved from multiple hours of crazy to 4 hours of conversation and coaching. You're spending strategic time with key adults and emerging young leaders. You're actually experiencing what you dreamed of all along. Spiritual growth in teens.

Realistic? Absolutely. And proven, too.

Did I mention the dozens of new adults praying for and pouring into young people? They have become your allies. Each with a personal ministry in the church and the name of one student attached to it. When you don't know how to possibly keep up on every kid, they provide extra sets of eyes and ears. When people in the congregation begin to grumble about the youth pastor, they come to the rescue. When complaints begin to surface about Kool-Aid® spilled on the Johnson Memorial Carpet, they point out the Jones Memorial Shop-Vac® in the church basement and suggest where to put it.

Problem solved.

Imagine. Youth ministry with cheerleaders.

As Ephesians 4:12 comes to life and young people are actually equipped and empowered to take risks and receive blessings, you gain more job security than you even dreamed. Your days of being a program director are over. New job description.

Mentor. Pastor. Shepherd. And friend.

Is that more like it?

When we make room, give away our tasks, and give teens a chance to try, fail, try again, and learn by doing, we emulate the example of Jesus.

He called youth to follow and then spent three plus years teaching them everything they would need to know before his earthly departure. You have just about that same amount of time before your kids go off into the world. Jesus was able to call his young protégés friends towards the end of their tutorial because they had learned enough to no longer be just students. They were ready.

Discipleship 101 done. Prerequisite finished.

Jesus was a mentor working himself out of a job. Literally. Teaching young followers to do greater things than they even witnessed while with him.

Because he gave them room, they could play their own game, call their own plays. Using his playbook and power. Instead of needing him to teach them the Word of God, he taught them how live it and understand it themselves. And teach others.

Do I really want you to quit your job? No. Just work yourself out of one. Understand it better and be better prepared to achieve a success so astounding the only explanation could ever be Jesus Christ. All because you have taken yourself off center stage, out of the spotlight. You have become invisible. Inevitably, you'll gain greater job security.

And keep from being fired. Ever.

It's simple. Spend only 4 hours monitoring young people who manage programs. Use the rest of your time mentoring people who mentor kids.

That's your real calling.

If you're a volunteer, you can have the same impact

as the paid person (sounds like an infomercial). As a part or full-time youth pastor, you'll be able to spend most of your time doing things that actually change lives—building relationships.

Instead of pointing to shelves filled with products **for** youth ministry, you can showcase products **of** youth ministry. Fruits of your labor. Blessed by God. Results of your efforts will be measurable by the number of youth actually doing the work of ministry.

The results of just 4 hours:

- See more adults involved in the right roles.

- Experience more youth being discipled and learning to serve.

- Watch more young people follow Jesus and find their place in his cause.

- See more youth supporting and working in their local church and community.

And guess what. All it takes to get on this path to paradigm shift is reading this book, following the directions, doing a few simple exercises, which all takes just…4 hours (feels like a theme or something).

You will have gone from doing youth ministry as program to doing it as relationship. You will be ready to mentor adults to mentor youth who take action for Jesus Christ.

Let's get ready to break the trap.

CHAPTER ONE

DEFINING SUCCESS

My friend, Benny Proffitt, founder of First Priority of America, turned me on to UCLA basketball legend, Coach John R. Wooden, a few years ago. Benny was a high school basketball coach turned youth pastor. The lessons he learned instructing boys on the hard court transferred to his approach to discipleship. Very effective. One of Benny's key influences was the late Coach Wooden and his Pyramid of Success.

As a 24-year-old high school English teacher, Wooden grew frustrated with the grading system he was required to use. He was compelled to help students better understand success as the result of effort. After years of perfecting his point of view, his famous pyramid-shaped diagram was completed in 1948. It gave an easy, visual explanation and way to measure efforts as success not just effects.

Simple. Practical.

Today, we also need a simple form of measurement. How do we gauge? What do we evaluate? How do we define success in youth work?

I remember sitting through a college class on qualification and quantification. Took me half the semester to understand the terms and keep them straight. At the moment, I thought Dr. Perrin was basically wasting our time. He wasn't.

What we do? Why we do it? How we measure it? Great questions to help us begin.

Much of my early ministry life was spent polishing. The weekly program I was responsible for creating took most of my time.

Maybe you can relate.

The majority of youth pastors I know today are caught in that trap and don't even know it. We find ourselves putting on a show. Possibly a performance. Not necessarily by design. But by accident.

At least I was.

If I had to break down the my hours, I can honestly say over 75% of my energy was used in three areas:

- Planning

- Preparing

- Polishing

My time, talent, and treasure was being used to build a program. I could blame it on expectations placed on me by my church, but that wouldn't be fair.

The congregation I was serving had never had a paid youth pastor. They figured I knew what to do to attract young people. Hired me for my expertise. Expected to see teens changed, transformed. Gave me a lot of freedom.

So why was I spending all my time away from youth planning events, activities, and meetings? I didn't sign up to be a program director. That wasn't my calling. But it became my means of measuring success.

A GLANCE BACK

I remember the season of my life when God called me to youth ministry. Ironically, I didn't really know what that vocation entailed, since I never had a youth pastor growing up.

During my teenage years, my dad was a church planter. There was no money in the budget for paid youth ministry staff. I recall a married couple who took us to some events occasionally, but overall, I didn't know what they did.

In my elementary and junior high years, there were some bible college students who worked with my dad as interns, but what a youth pastor was and what were they supposed to do left me clueless.

Ironic. Called to something I didn't understand.

Despite my ignorance of the definition of a youth

pastor, I knew I wanted to help young people. Giving teens a chance to discover who they were in their adolescent years tugged at my heart. I could articulate that desire. Just didn't know how.

My own teen years were filled with less than good decisions (ok, some bad decisions). Not because I didn't have a solid family. Or because I wasn't exposed to the message of God's Word or the love of Jesus Christ. My home was a safe, healthy, Christian experience. The Word of God was honored. Jesus was lifted up as Savior and Lord.

But something was still missing.

As I look back and think of the transitions I underwent relocating from one state, school, or community to another as a teen, I think moving was a huge factor. It certainly contributed to many of my poor choices. Yet, despite the teenage turmoil, I was a pretty secure young man.

My personal confidence not withstanding, I was still on a quest to be somebody. That didn't necessarily mean illusions of fame or fortune. I was just looking some level of significance, but to find it meant I had to find a way to fit in wherever I went.

Did I mention bad decisions?

Over the next few years, I began to discover insights I'm still pondering to this very day. For me. And for those I serve. A truth that guides my life, my family. And the ministry outside my home.

You don't need to fit in once you realize you belong.

I didn't comprehend that belonging is knowing who you are and living it. Not ignoring who are you and hiding it. Just getting by. Being lost. Big difference between the two ideas. There was a gap between my being and my doing that existed simply to mask my lack of knowing. Lack of understanding. I was looking. Searching. Faking it. And getting more and more lost at the same time.

And I wasn't alone.

Hallways and homes were (and always have been) filled with youth wondering about life and wandering through their days hoping to 'find themselves.'

Countless young people in my world were just like me. Looking for a safe place to land. Settling for artificial significance. Literally dying to true self, denying their worth, and destroying the best they had to offer the world to please a few others they called friends.

I was putting on a performance. Living a lie.

A hard to way to exist. I knew the pain of it all, but didn't understand its power over me. All I believed is that no young person should have to deal with the void I felt. My calling from God was to do something about that problem for other people—young people.

When Jesus warns us in John 10 about an enemy who comes to kill and destroy, I think my teenage struggle and confusion was the essence of what he was describing. His words allude to the same lie, the first lie, that Satan told Eve in the Garden of Eden. The serpent polished a piece of fruit, slithered up to her, and posed a devastating question.

"Did God really say…?"

Let the mind games begin.

From the beginning of humankind, the liar has been trying to confuse us, convince us that we must do something to be significant. We must put on an act. Apologize for our being.

He planted a seed in human DNA suggesting we don't belong as created. No. We must fit in. Being offspring of the Creator isn't good enough.

Try harder.

The world teaches us to question not only our significance. But our very existence. The fallen nature we have inherited leaves us unaware of who we are and whose we are. As we enter a sinful world in human deficit, the tragedy is that we don't know that God believes in us. We are his children.

The lie continues generation to generation.

From Eve to us.

CONFUSED ABOUT MY CALL

So there I was. 20-years-old. Ready or not for youth ministry and really not ready at all. I didn't exactly know what this calling entailed. I couldn't precisely describe what I was missing during my teen years. I certainly didn't know what I needed to give those younger than me now in my care.

So I planned a program. Pretty typical overall.

- Big Sunday night meetings
- Wednesday night bible studies
- Weekend leadership retreats
- Summer camp experiences
- Trips to concerts and conferences
- Lock-ins and overnight events
- Lunches on the school campuses
- Mission trips and service projects

You get the idea.

My job was to create an experience that would attract young people. Open their eyes to the gospel. Get them to respond to Jesus Christ. The greater the numbers, the greater the conversion rate.

The more effort I contributed to creating something spectacular, the more salvations we would eventually see.

Made sense. Somewhat.

And without realizing it, I had defined success as size. The bigger the better. Tada!

A few years ago, a friend shared his secret of success with me. This man had built an enterprise, and I was curious about how. "Tim, you have to know your product. Create distribution channels. Perfect the manufacturing process. But build your business backward. Begin with the end in mind. That's it."

Seemed simple.

My end goal was simple. See more teens in love with Jesus. My means was to create a dynamic program.

Sounded pure enough. So I followed this process.

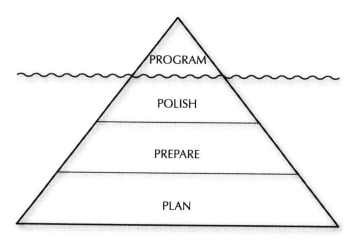

That was my pyramid. Program was the pinnacle of success, so I took ¾ of my time to make sure everything was perfect. Spend the majority of my time planning. Lay a well-thought through foundation. Refine the plan, as I made preparations. Cross every t. Dot every i. Lots of preparation allowed me to be flexible in case the Holy Spirit might just show up with an idea of his own. Then I would make it pretty. Put on the final touches and polish it until it shined.

Of course kids would come. There was no other program like it nearby. Not to mention I was the only youth pastor for 30 miles.

Everything you could imagine in the spectrum of youth work was included. I missed very little. Caught every new trend. Read every magazine. If it was leading-edge, I knew about it.

The ministry offered something for everyone. It certainly looked impressive. There were new ideas. New faces. New decisions being made for Christ. We outgrew our meeting place. Moved operations outside the church. Opened a killer youth center.

And just kept on growing.

Crowds **and** conversions. A winning combo.

To top it all off, we were expanding. Churches were asking how to get the same results. Using the model. Replicating the method. Even wearing the brand.

But without knowing it, we were on the verge of failure. Even though our efforts were a mile wide, the effects were an inch deep.

I would soon experience the same devastation that research would indicate well-over a decade later. Like the rest of the body of Christ, over 80% of the young people active in our ministry would eventually walk away from the church. And their faith.

What appeared to be success to some still left young

people wanting more. Even though they confessed Christ and came every week, we weren't seeing real transformation and regeneration.

I was striking out.

The best illustration I have found to represent the exodus rate of youth from the church comes from the game of baseball. A term called the Mendoza Line.

Mario Mendoza was a Major League Baseball player in the 1970's who struggled at bat. He averaged about .200 at the plate. Far below an acceptable performance in the major league. In 1979, Mario's average was calculated at .198. Barely good enough to justify his position with the Pittsburg Pirates. How could they keep him on the roster? Was his defensive game good enough to turn a blind eye to his inability to score? Eventually, his career ended in 1982, but not before the Mendoza Line became the measure for poor batting in the world of baseball.

The correlation between Mendoza and my youth ministry was evident. I was batting below .200 no matter how hard I was swinging.

Was I conscious of my measurement of success? Not at all. I was just following the techniques of others who were touted as the few really doing it well.

Some ideas I copied. Others I created. All in hopes of drawing youth. Not to a program. To Jesus Christ. But in the end, what people noticed most was the effect. Everyone seemed to like the show. Made a fuss. Even attended most of the time.

Occasionally, I got a hold of a fast ball and hit it out of the park. But the lasting effect was short-lived.

EXERCISE

In the space below, write your definition of ministry success.

_____

_____

_____

When you look at a youth ministry in another church, what impresses you? Write down the three things you envy most.

1. _____
2. _____
3. _____

What are you most proud of about the program you lead? Be specific. Choose one aspect you would be afraid to lose.

_____

_____

_____

ESCAPE

Make a list of everything you do in youth ministry on a weekly basis. It doesn't matter if your paid or volunteer. Look at each activity and assign a value to it. On a scale of 1-10, determine if it is essential to spiritual growth in young people. Then write down how much time that tasks requires.

To escape the trap of full-time ministry, it is vital we remove all responsibilities that have little (less the 7 on the scale) impact on making disciples as Jesus instructed.

TASK	1 TO 10	TIME
_____	_____	_____
_____	_____	_____
_____	_____	_____
_____	_____	_____
_____	_____	_____
_____	_____	_____

DOWNLOAD WORKSHEETS AT 4HOURYOUTHMINISTRY.COM

NOTES

After praying about the previous chapter, take a moment to write down ideas or convictions that God is communicating. Listen to his leading. Guard yourself. The enemy is going to lie to you.

CHAPTER TWO

RE-DEFINING SUCCESS

Coach Wooden found out the hard way that the industry standard for measuring success in the education world was flawed. It took him 14 years to eventually identify 25 behaviors that would define his idea of success.

I was also discovering something about the standards of measuring success in the youth ministry industry and embarking on the same journey. It would also take me years to uncover secrets of sorts along the way. Truths about how Jesus actually changes lives.

The church I was serving at the time split. I was part of the collateral damage. Cindy and I had relocated from metro Minneapolis to rural Michigan for this position. She was teaching school, but I was without a job. Wasn't sure what to do. I had an even greater passion for youth. But no real platform now.

Time to regroup. On my knees.

Henry Blackaby's book, Experiencing God, was the popular read of the day. It had sat on my shelves for some time now. Too long.

Time for me to read it.

I remember the first day I knelt in my home during that time of searching. The same room I'm writing in tonight. A simple prayer would guide my quiet time for weeks to come. It was short and to the point.

"God, please show me where you're working and how to join you there."

I coupled that petition with another prayer my dad had taught me, when I first entered pastoral ministry.

"Lord, help me dream only the biggest dreams you will bless." A prayer I still plead to this day.

I didn't want to waste one ounce of energy. One moment of time. One penny of provision chasing anything that wasn't from him. Anything he wouldn't mark with his blessing.

This was a watershed moment for me. One I didn't want to waste. My heart was pure. I was asking God for his plan, his process, his direction.

Specifically for youth ministry.

His answer would be made complete in time, but it began that summer in prayer. Morning after morning in a position of submission, I reiterated the same request, "God, please show me where you're working and how to join you there. Help me dream only the biggest dreams you will bless."

In my heart, I knew God had spoken his desire to me. Revealed his heart. There was no mistaken. He was clear. I knew he was uniting the Christian youth of the world. Once again, I sensed his leading. Passion was mounting. I got up, called advisors, started praying and making plans. And shared the voice of God and vision I sensed with the few youth I still served in the local community.

That was brand new.

A change in strategy. A redefinition of success was on the rise in my heart. It would take root soon.

Instead of revealing my ministry plans to young people and seeking their approval, I was sharing what God had said with them. **With teens.** I was including them. Not in a program. In the planning. Treating them like coequals in the kingdom of God.

In the past, I would plan, prepare, polish, and present. Then gain their support. Get them to adopt my ministry child. My mode of operation was to create enough hype they couldn't help but pretend to like the idea. I spent hours and days at a time dreaming and scheming knowing that with enough salesmanship, they would buy into my ministry.

This time was different. Without consciously recognizing it, I had engaged young people in the process. From the beginning. We began to plan.

Together.

From conception. To completion. They would have

significant involvement. A new means of measurement was being developed. How I used my time.

The abrupt lack of congregational backing, building, or budget I now faced forced me to reconsider my philosophy of youth ministry as well.

God has not only opened my eyes to what he was doing, he opened the door for me learn how to join him. Effectively. He answered my prayer. Far beyond my knowledge. Or understanding.

He removed a barrier I never knew existed.

It was youth ministry.

CONFESSIONS OF A PROGRAM JUNKIE

Ever been addicted to anything? No one plans for it to happen. It sneaks up on you and takes control before you realize. And you can't quit until you admit.

CHAPTER TWO

Dr. Phil puts it this way in rule #4 of his life lessons: "You can't change what you do not acknowledge."

God was transforming my point of view and my priorities. I started to realize I was addicted to youth ministry programming. An issue I was beginning to confess. Not only did I have a problem, I possessed all the paraphernalia.

- ☑ Ponytail. Check.

- ☑ Earrings. Check, check.

- ☑ Guitar. Check.

- ☑ Cool fish tank. Check.

- ☑ Electric dartboard. Check.

- ☑ Entire YS® Ideas Library. Check.

All I was missing was a cool Hebrew tattoo.

Between a few years of formal education, ministry conventions and conferences, and the advice of veterans, I was a full-blown, full-time youth pastor spending the better part of my week in an office, behind a desk. Writing lessons. Planning events. Creating games. Even contemplating shaving my head.

That's where all my effort went.

I was doing whatever it took to get young people to show up to ***my*** ministry. I was clearly a program junkie. Creating logos, apparel, youth group names. It transpired by accident. Had to transform on purpose. I needed to overcome my obsession.

My perspective was changing.

My protocol had to follow.

You ever break an addiction? Codependency. Drugs. Tobacco. Porn. Doritos®. Addiction is a disease. A neurological disorder. And I'm not making light of it by making the correlation to youth ministry.

This is a serious matter.

Program had become a synthetic substitute. Meetings had become an artificial replacement for real, authentic relationships.

I was determined to break free from my newly recognized need for a fix. It wouldn't be easy because it was part of my life for some time, but I had a plan. This wasn't my first addiction in life, so I had a few ideas on how to overcome the habit.

There wasn't a 12-step program for youth pastors (although it might be a good idea to create), but I did need to make some strategic decisions. Because redefining success required it.

So I created my own.

STEPS TO RECOVERY

- First, I admitted my shortcomings. I was powerless. My ministry was unmanageable.

- Second, I believed God had a plan. Only he could provide the power to restore my sanity.

- Third, I sought amends for my decision to hijack the ministry and gave youth ownership.

- Fourth, I made an account of my tasks and time and determined what was essential.

- Finally, I went public and shared my new approach to ministry with all who would listen.

I am a recovering youth ministry addict.

Not recovered.

Addiction can be deadly. Before you even realize

you're relapsing, you can get sucked back into the lifestyle. And it can destroy you.

In the beginning of my metamorphosis, I had to be careful not to feed my newly broken habit. Refraining from certain establishments, conversations, and gatherings was crucial to my early stages of recovery.

- No more buying youth ministry books. All those publications on games, lesson ideas, and service projects were killing me. It became apparent how all those resources could best be utilized. I would let kids use them from now on. They were now in charge of planning events. Maybe they could use these tools to jump-start their ideas.

- No more youth ministry conventions. The worst place for a recovering addict to be is in a room full of thousands of other addicts.

> Dangerous. The favorite question asked, "So how many kids are in your ministry?" is like putting pot in a pipe while holding a lit match. I would have to stay clear.
>
> - No more subscriptions to periodicals that reminded me of big programs. I was breaking the habit, and the last thing I needed to be reading was youth ministry 'porn' that showed airbrushed pictures of unrealistic outcomes. Articles that created a fantasy worldview of youth ministry only a few churches would ever experience.

My little 'Steps to Recovery' shtick might sound like a stretch, but it wasn't far from the truth for me. There is a little fiction mixed in for your reading pleasure in the last few paragraphs, but I undoubtedly felt the pull of an addiction to return to doing youth ministry like I had for years.

I was fighting a compulsion to program. Go back to following my little "P-Pyramid" even though I knew there must be a better way. So I paused and took the time to take another inventory.

As I reviewed the past few years, I discovered something profound (or at least blatantly obvious). The kids who showed signs of real, lasting spiritual development were those I spent the most time with.

God was granting me greater understand. To reach more kids required more time. Not so hard to grasp.

When God eliminated my youth ministry program, he lopped off a liability and left me with real assets.

Relationships!

The minute I was left with nothing but relationships was the moment I desperately needed most. I found myself the proud owner of an invaluable resource, and I didn't even know it was in my possession (kind of like youth pastor meets American Pickers, Pawn Stars, or Antiques Road Show).

The light began to go on. Success was making sense.

IT'S ALL ABOUT RELATIONSHIPS

The greatest evangelist I have ever met happens to be my father. From truck driver to church planter, he was a fanatic for the cross. Still is today.

The secret of his ministry success was his golf game. Average at best. It was not his swing or course management but his consistency that made his game valuable. He spent Wednesdays on the back nine. Not with pastors. Not with believers. Or church members. With a non-Christian garbage man named, Doug. My dad built relationships on the green. That was his pastoral strategy. He knew the value of time.

I'm not sure John Maxwell said it first, but he often gets the credit. Either way, my dad quoted somebody time and time again. And lived the words, "People will never care how much you know until they know how much you care."

I'll never forget that phrase. Not because it's catchy.

But because it's true.

My new definition of success was coming into focus. I could even begin to articulate it.

"Lives are changed through relationships, and relationships that change lives take time."

A paradigm shift.

A new pyramid of success. There was a way to measure after all. Efforts. Not effects.

Time with teens would determine the direction of the ministry. They would learn by doing, discover God's plan for their lives, and grow spiritually. Giving them my time more consistently and releasing ownership over to them was the key to managing ministry.

For God to work, I had to let go. End bad habits. And begin new ones.

Healthier ones.

EXERCISE

Let's go shopping. Really. I want you to stop reading and go to the store. Time for a taste test.

Sneak down to your favorite grocer and find your way to the frozen food aisle. We're buying ice cream! Two kinds. The cheap stuff. And the good stuff.

How do you tell the difference? The junk brand says 'artificially flavored' right on the front of the container. The yummy kind doesn't. Cheap is also complicated. Just turn the box over and read the ingredients for yourself. Yowza!

Could you pronounce half of that crap? Me either. Now, read what's included in the premium package. Simple, huh? That's what we're creating in 4 hours a week. Simple. Relationships. That's where lives are changed and God's Word becomes real. It's the way Jesus did ministry. It should be our way, too.

Are there artificial flavorings in your ministry?

ESCAPE

Time to expand your list. The items you wrote down at the end of Chapter One may be necessary, but necessarily done by you. Young people learn by doing, just like you. But unless they learn to lead in the church, they leave it in search of something or someone who values what they have to offer the world today.

Write down your list again. This time, prayerfully consider the young people within your influence and assign each task to a name. A teen. If you teach them, they can learn to do your job. After all, teaching them their role in the church is your job.

TASK	NAME
_____	_____
_____	_____
_____	_____
_____	_____
_____	_____
_____	_____

DOWNLOAD WORKSHEETS AT 4HOURYOUTHMINISTRY.COM

NOTES

After praying about the previous chapter, take a moment to write down ideas or convictions that God is communicating. Listen to his leading. Guard yourself. The enemy is going to lie to you.

CHAPTER THREE

RESTRUCTURING TIME

The value of time was making more sense and really sinking in for me. Not necessarily to the people watching though. I wasn't spending much time in an office sitting behind a desk, so keeping tabs on me was tough.

"No office hours? What does Tim do anyway?"

I had the same amount of time as before, but I was

managing it differently. A skill no one ever mentioned. A youth ministry seminar I must have missed. Or an article I apparently overlooked. The 'Smarter Not Harder' study series passed me by.

I was now involved in a new church plant. As the pastor no less. Leading a local youth ministry still. Coaching high school golf. And the father of two young sons. Time was limited to say the least. And I obviously didn't know how to say, "No!"

So I had to reorganize my organizer to do the 'Big Rock' thing I had read about from Steven Covey. The hardest part was determining what went in my ministry jar and what didn't.

Remember my moment of realization that lives are changed through relationships, and relationships that change lives take time? That rule now guided my decisions. Everything else fit around relationships.

My means of measuring ministry effectiveness would take a new form. I was taking more time to build relationships, which left **no time** for planning. At the end of the day, I had little energy to wonder what Wednesday night would look like. So I didn't.

Programs took a backseat to people.

My new priority was getting into young peoples' lives. Their schedules determined mine. Not the other way around, as had been the case. They were no longer expected to attend anything they didn't help plan. And I was bending over backward to see the best in them, which basically meant I had to learn to ignore what they wanted me to see in order to recognize their real potential. Possibilities I never noticed were present before.

The more I learned to overlooked the oddities in teens, the more I cherished those people who chose to disregard my dumb decisions and adolescent choices, too. Like God does for all of us.

Getting intimately involved with young people also meant going deeper. Seeing beneath the surface.

BELOW THE WATERLINE

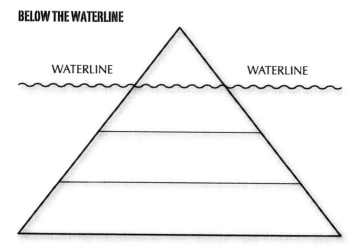

The more I thought about it, the more Coach John Wooden's pyramid resembled an iceberg. As I reflected on the lessons I had learned from these floating wonders, I saw a new model unfold.

As you may or may not know, 90% of the ice mass lies below the surface of the water. The unseen share is actually what forms the shape and supports the visible. If the structure below the waterline deteriorates, the 10% falls apart.

Even fails to exist.

This may be a common illustration, but don't pass over it too quickly. This isn't elemental.

It's fundamental.

The word picture is paramount to creating a 4-Hour Youth Ministry where your valuable time is used more efficiently doing the right things. And doing them more effectively. Don't miss the apparent in search of something more sophisticated only to bypass the basics of this point.

Human nature tends to see the visible and draw

conclusions. We value the viewable. We're drawn to the dynamic.

Due to its very stature, the tip of the iceberg stands tall and glimmers in the sun. Its magnificence reflected in the water. Amazing to behold. And hard for anyone to ignore. Spectacular too see.

Much like polished programs I spent years creating, the iceberg gets people's attention. Because it is obvious even to the oblivious. You can't help but notice it's breathtaking beauty.

God's word to Samuel is relevant for this revelation. "For the LORD sees not as man sees: man looks on the outward appearance, but the LORD looks on the heart." (1 Samuel 16:7 ESV).

When Israel was looking for a king, God sent Samuel on a scavenger hunt for hierarchy. Like us, his eyes shifted toward shape. Fixed on figure and form.

But like Samuel, we must also go beneath the seen. And that requires fighting our tendency to be impressed with appearance.

Without taking a look below the surface, we never see the source. The strength. We only see the face. The ever-changing facade. Or end-product. Not the heart. Or the basis of character.

As I write, I am reminded of God the Father. The unseen. Created seen. People look at creation. Bewildered by its beauty. Miss the Creator. Because the seen is spectacular to behold. And they worship the created instead. That's backward but true for many.

Paul's words to the church in 2 Corinthians 4:18 come to mind as I consider the value of the invisible. "So we fix our eyes not on what is seen, but on what is unseen. For what is seen is temporary, but what is unseen is eternal."

Too much importance placed on the perceptible not the potential. The temporal. Instead of the eternal.

One of the greatest lessons of our faith is faith itself.

"Now faith is the substance of things hoped for, the evidence of things not seen." (Hebrews 11:1 NIV).

In the past, I was enamored with nonessentials. Programs that looked impressive took the greatest portion of my time to build. Only later to find out they didn't produce effects equal to my efforts.

The idea of investing my time in relationships below the waterline where real development occurs in young lives was revolutionary (to me). While very few people witnessed what I was doing or noticed where I spent my days, God was accomplishing more than I could ever imagine. He was doing the work. I was just follow Jesus' example. Doing life with young people. And teaching along the way.

That was the essence of my ministry. My presence in the office was virtually non-existent, and I was seeing greater results than ever before in the lives of students. There was no time for me to focus on planning a program.

And no need.

THE B-PYRAMID™

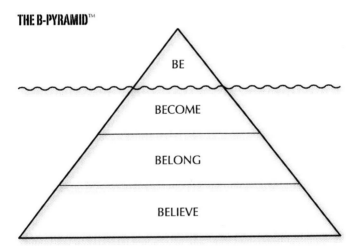

The process of planning, preparing, and polishing I explained in Chapter One worked to establish an exciting program. And for many years, I settled. Called it success. So did others who observed it up close. And from afar.

What they witnessed on the surface, above the waterline, was enough for most to marvel. But down deep (no pun intended) I knew it didn't measure up to God's standards. Young people were not meant to be spectators of youth ministry as my colleague, Rick Mills, communicates in his book, The Big Turnover.

Go beneath in order to go beyond. Wade in past what was comfortable. Get out of the shallows.

If the unseen in the natural world forms the seen, could it be much different for the supernatural? Did God differentiate his ways from one corner of creation to the next? Or did he follow a pattern?

My friend, Gary Perritt, often reminds me that God works in process and order. Not chaos. Everything is procedural. Fits in place. Progressive.

I had definitely adhered to a process, but it wasn't necessarily right. Just because it was orderly and growing didn't mean it was Godly. Or even biblical.

A few years ago, my wife, Cindy, began to articulate it this way. She challenged my thinking with these words. **"When we put our passion in front of God's plan, we bypass his provision."**

I was blinded by my own enthusiasm. And sidestepping God's strategy. His plan for making disciples was relational not organizational. Certainly not programmatic, which had become problematic for me.

Programs didn't change lives. Gatherings didn't bring growth. Meetings and ministry are not synonyms.

My planning process didn't work. But I needed a simple visual. Some sort of reminder of how to best

CHAPTER THREE

put my new priorities into practice.

On a napkin in Orlando, Florida, God showed me a diagram that demonstrated how people grow spiritually to become what he intended for them from the beginning. This diagram keeps me in check and keeps God in control.

And it keeps me connected to my real calling.

As you can see on page 78, the B-Pyramid™ has four levels. Three of which quantify efforts. The fourth one qualifies effects.

Starting at the bottom, well-below the surface or line of sight, in quiet conversations and private appointments, I would begin to build a base. Broaden my influence. The majority of my week would be spent with people.

No exceptions.

If I failed to build relationships, I failed.

No excuses.

When I reviewed the previous way I measured ministry effectiveness, it came in the form of the ever-popular attendance sheet (now software for some). That single piece of paper that tracks whether young people showed up or not. It was my lifeline in the past. My job security in many ways.

If the sheet wasn't full, I might not be full-time either. From Sunday school to Wednesday night bible study and every other event in between, attendance was crucial and calculated. And then presented to the pastor and church board. On the third Thursday of each month, I put my job and neck on the line when I passed out copies. Men and women who never attended one meeting or darkened the door of a youth ministry event would pass judgment based upon nothing but a few numbers.

CHAPTER THREE

Can I get cynical for a moment?

[When did attendance become the benchmark for success in the church? Sure. It indicates the size of a crowd, but that's about all it really measures. And just because people are showing up doesn't mean they're growing up in Christ.]

Still I greatly believe in quantifying. The right things. Real results. So how would I record relationships and manage my time with teens without losing track?

A new benchmark would become necessary to trace my steps with students. But not attendance.

I would track contact and connections in four ways:

- **TYPE 1:** Personal
- **TYPE 2:** Group
- **TYPE 3:** Verbal
- **TYPE 4:** Written

My first goal was to make sure that one-on-one communication took place intentionally. Standing next to a young man at the urinal on Sunday morning couldn't count. It would need to be a scheduled meeting on their turf. In their world. And it should happen often for every young person.

The next tactic was also life-on-life, but instead of individual connection it would come in the form of small group. I would make sure to spend time with a young person and their friends. It might be after school sitting in bleachers, in the park skating, or just sharing a cappuccino or Coke®.

Personal or community connection was best, but time was limited. And there must be more links to young lives. Picking up the phone would be the next contact point. Just a brief verbal conversation would add to my growing association. I might call to encourage them to study hard for tomorrow's exams or to let them know I noticed they sat the bench at last night's ball game. Just recognizing realities in their lives. Not badger, hound, and nag them for missing last week's youth meeting.

And finally, a written note would top it all off. A postcard. Email. Letter. Sometimes serious. Or light to create a laugh. Today, it's even easier with social media sites opening doors to teens who share their lives online for the world to see.

The plan was too easy. Ignore weekly attendance at events and meetings. Even worship. Focus on keeping the Connect boxes full. In 3 months, each one should contain ***at least*** one ✗ per student.

NAME	CONNECT				ATTENDANCE				
OWEN	✗	✗	✗	✗					
BRIAN	✗	✗	✗	✗					
MEGAN	✗	✗	✗	✗					
ALICIA	✗	✗	✗	✗					
JAMES	✗	✗	✗	✗					

And as the connections increased, so did attendance. If I made sure the first four boxes were full, I didn't have to worry about the rest. They looked like this most of the time.

NAME	CONNECT				ATTENDANCE				
OWEN	X	X	X	X	X	X	X	X	X
BRIAN	X	X	X	X	X	X	X	X	X
MEGAN	X	X	X	X	X	X	X	X	X
ALICIA	X	X	X	X	X	X	X	X	X
JAMES	X	X	X	X	X	X	X	X	X

It was the initial stage in making the B-Pyramid™ practical. Get involved. Connect.

And find myself doing less.

God doing more.

EXERCISE

You have to **make marks** to make marks on young lives. This simple cliché works to help create a 4-Hour Youth Ministry.

On the chart below, list the names of young people involved in the youth program you serve. Don't just record the regular youth who you consider the core. List the fringe kids, too.

Ignore the Attendance column. Just mark down how many times in the last 3 months you have intentionally connected outside weekly meetings or events with these youth.

NAME	CONNECT				ATTENDANCE				

DOWNLOAD WORKSHEETS AT 4HOURYOUTHMINISTRY.COM

ESCAPE

syn·o·nym

[**sin**-*uh*-nim]

–noun

1. a word having the same or nearly the same meaning as another in the language, as *joyful, elated, glad*.

To break free from the trap of full-time youth ministry and experience the joy that comes from using 4 hours more efficiently and effectively requires a language lesson.

Take a moment to answer these questions in all seriousness.

If a dead bolt was placed on the youth room door and you were not allowed to have large group meetings, events, or activities for 6 months, what would your ministry look like now? How would you influence young people, since meeting and ministry are not synonyms?

Your answer will guide and direct the your future with youth.

NOTES

After praying about the previous chapter, take a moment to write down ideas or convictions that God is communicating. Listen to his leading. Guard yourself. The enemy is going to lie to you.

CHAPTER FOUR

UNDERSTANDING THE B-PYRAMID™

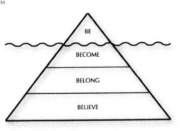

Look back over your life, and you'll discover God at work. Through relationships. Dissect your own discipleship, and discover people not programs having the most impact on your faith development.

Take a few minutes to really review your faith journey, and you'll recall names not catchy summer camp themes or Sunday school lessons.

Pastor Jim Graham and C. David Bass.

Other than my parents, my brothers, and my wife, Cindy, those are the first two people I remember who made a real difference. They were men who loved me enough to draw lines, define boundaries, drop their agendas, and let me dream.

They didn't just spend time with me. They invested time it. And over time I learned. In relationship.

If we go back to the beginning, we learn something about the power of relationship and proximity. Adam had it first. A personal relationship with the Creator in paradise. But soon God revealed a new truth to man. He was alone. His personal proximity to Adam brought the realization that man needed companionship. A relationship with another of his own kind. And a union that created completion and provided accountability that couldn't be counterfeit or contrived. It couldn't be formed through program. It had to be fashioned through a rib. It must be life-on-life.

God made Eve.

Young people who are discovering their identity in this difficult world need the security of someone on their side, too. Someone to raise the bar. And help them reach it. Someone to be there when the enemy raises his ugly head and raises the question of their meaning with the same age-old lie Eve heard.

"Did God really say…?"

They need to know that a person they can look up to and admire believes in them just like they are. They need to belong. Not just fit in. And they need the chance to become who God intended. That includes having multiple chances to try, fail, and try again if necessary. And a hand to pick them up if they fall.

Over time, God had been teaching me why all the stuff I was doing didn't work long-term. Why my great program years earlier yielded less than 20% of life-time disciples. Below .200. He shared the secret I was looking for in the second chapter of Genesis.

"It is not good for man to be alone."

The first time I really paid much attention to that verse was in a weekend retreat in Austin, Texas, hosted by Josh McDowell. He had invited some close friends to spend a few days discussing the idea of inter-generational youth ministry. Our speaker was Dr. David Ferguson, from Intimate Life Ministries.

David suggested that Genesis 2:18 was the first revelation God ever gave man. The moment he let Adam in on a little secret. Something he had not known before. He was alone.

Like you and me, Adam needed companionship.

Someone who could understand, empathize, accept. Remind him he was a regent, prince, son of God.

Did you know that we aren't born believing in our true identity? We don't know who we are in Christ until someone shares that information, and we choose to accept. Only two people ever had that privilege. They had the best opportunity for success ever. And even they slipped. What chance do their descendants have? Especially teens smack dab in the stages of development and discovery.

The lie Adam and Eve fell for still lives on. Most people define themselves not by who they really are as God's offspring. But by what they do. Vocation. Location. Livelihood.

By what people see on the surface of our lives.

It is the same with institutions. We judge by what we see on the outside. The name. The brand on the sign.

It's similar with churches. They are known for their services. Their events. Their edifices. And it applies to pastors, too. Many youth pastors define their life, their ministry, their success by the programs they lead. We care what people think, and people typically draw their conclusions by what they see. Fair? No, but true. Reminds us to never judge a book by it's cover. But we do.

It is reasonable to say that we buy Eden's lie. What's inside is not enough. We want more. To be more like God. But since we can't, we pretend and create what people consider spectacular from pure perception.

If that's not bad enough, we also overlook the first revelation Adam heard. For thousands of years. We do ministry alone. Most of our time us spent separated from those we serve. Good intentions. Poor plan.

Being alone is isolation. Isolation removes accountability. There are times we find value in a form of alone we call solitude. Luke 5 tells us that Jesus often withdrew to lonely places, but it was his intentional time to regroup, building relationship with his father. Lonely places force us to rely upon God for strength, but too much aloneness creates exclusion.

And aloneness is a plague.

Ever notice when people get in trouble the most? When they're alone. Our students make poor decisions alone. Youth pastors dabble into danger when they're alone as well. Clergy cave. Alone doesn't' work. It's still not good.

For people to believe in who they are as a child of the King born with birthrights than can't be taken away, they need someone to believe in them first. Believing in who we are, what we can become, and who God intended us to be is bestowed upon us.

CHAPTER FOUR

By someone.

Layer by layer, the B-Pyramid™ provides the structure for allocating time and building healthy relationships. It helps break down our schedules, establish priorities, and use time more wisely.

How does the pyramid work?

BELIEVE

How can you tell when someone believes in you?

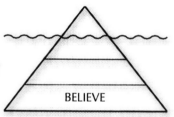

Yesterday, I spent another afternoon at a high school cross country meet. Cindy says cross the happiest place on earth. It certainly is a much different atmosphere than other sporting events. Every kid is celebrated. From the first girl who runs across the line at 19:04 to the last boy who walks across in 32:46. People cheer. Celebrate.

Believing starts with showing up. There's nothing I can do as a father more important than stop what I'm doing to show up and watch my sons run. Or someone else's sons. Or daughters. I am amazed race after face to see young people line up, look around, and realize mom, dad, grandma, guardian, no one showed up to watch.

Believe begins by being there.

As a youth pastor, I have kids in my care whose parents either or not available or are just irresponsible. Cindy asked a boy last week whether his dad could make it to a meet. His answer, "No, cross country is just not his thing."

Not his thing?

Heartbreaking.

Parents, pastors, teachers, whoever. It doesn't have to

be our thing. It's their thing. That's what matters. And when we simply show up, we say, "I believe in you."

We can't be too busy to be involved.

But sometimes that's exactly the case. I was spending all my time as a youth pastor on my stuff in hopes that they would show up. But all young people wanted was for me to abandon my thing for theirs. I was too busy doing the wrong stuff with excellence.

Let's look at Jesus as our ministry model. His methods jump off the page, when we determine the need to emulate his approach to discipleship.

In particular, let's take a look at how he spent his time. Specifically, where did Jesus show up?

- **Earth.** This is no small point to overlook. Jesus determined to come hang out on our turf. Not expect us to come to his place or rise to his level. He left the comfort of his heavenly home and offered to meet in our world. Not his office, youth center, or church.

- ***Events.*** We see Jesus everywhere from celebrations and ceremonies. From weddings to funerals. Jesus spent time in real life situations. Went where people lived. As part of the local community.

- ***Environment.*** Jesus walked into places where people shopped, worked, played. Everyday situations in normal and natural settings. From fishing to feasting. Tax collecting to temple worship.

Throughout Jesus' ministry, we see him eating, drinking, living where real people hung out. He didn't miss the important events of others to accomplish his own agenda. Read the gospels. Witness Jesus with and within the world his students already knew. Places they called home.

Time for me to adjust my ministry mind-set even more. Working in isolation would never create value, influence, or disciples. I must leave my world to enter theirs. Too simple to ignore.

There was no biblical evidence of my previous model. Jesus never intentionally created an event. He never said, "Hey, Peter, get out your guitar and draw a crowd." Using my time to build a program was a waste. Poor stewardship. Irresponsible.

But it feels good. Feels right. Everyone does it. That's how we measure success.

A few years ago, I agreed to consult a church who was rebuilding their youth program. The pastor and I spent a few hours on the phone over a few weeks. Time and time again, I emphasized the value of process over product. Discipleship as a relationship that takes time. Growth comes through experience, learning happens best by doing. Youth need the chance to make decisions, make mistakes, make messes. Through trial and error, they discover their gifts, hone their skills, and recognize their significance in Christ and in his cause.

The pastor agreed, so I flew in for a couple of days to meet with the church leadership team. Department heads who oversaw staff, programs, and ministries were assembled at a location away from the church. Ironically, I met with everyone with a title you could possibly imagine.

Except the youth pastor.

The church hired a really gifted young guy because of his creativity. His task was to build a program that could attract youth. The very thing this congregation needed to lose was included in his job description.

His days were spent in an office dreaming and scheming. If there was a new youth ministry idea surfacing anywhere, it probably filled his head or was floating on his desk.

He clearly had a youth ministry problem. Program junkie. And the pastor recognized it.

The church leadership was now prayerfully convicted that youth most be the owner / operators of youth ministry, but they just hired this youth pastor 6 months earlier. He relocated his family and was undoubtably doing what they originally expected.

In all fairness, he deserved a chance to change. But after 6 more months of watching from the wings, it was apparent change was not possible for him.

They made a hard decision. Paid him a hefty severance. And sent him on his way. Started looking for someone who loved young people enough to leave the office and let go of their own program.

Believe begins by being there. It is where relationships take root, nurture begins, and growth occurs.

BELONG

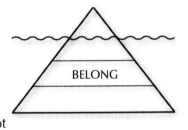

You always know where my wife is sitting at a school sporting event. She's the one yelling. Not at referees. Not at coaches. Not criticisms.

Cindy makes sure every young person on the court, course, or field hears their name multiple times during a game, race, or event. That's her rule. She acquired the idea when our boys began attending Kanakuk Kamps, in Branson, Missouri, years ago. Dr. Joe White, President of Kanakuk Ministries, has taught his staff this simple means of making young people feel valued. Mention their name. Often. And in a positive manner.

As young people begin to recognize you believe in them, something amazing takes place. They believe in themselves, too. But it takes time. And repetition. Doesn't happen in a weekend, in an hour, or typically in a crowd.

My tendency is to go out of my way to make time. Cross the room to have a conversation. And include some healthy touch. Show up and show an interest.

But that is not my character.

I have to be intentional to show others I believe in them. Dropping notes, compliments, or appointments doesn't come naturally to me. It's not my bent. I have to work at it to be honest.

More times than I care to confess, I would rather remain in my office. That's my comfort zone, but it doesn't accomplish my calling. Jesus says, "Go." Get uncomfortable, go deeper to make disciples.

As we believe by showing up, belonging takes place. Confidence grows. Because you take the time to show young people you believe in them as they are, where they are, and they feel good about themselves. You didn't ask them to fit in, change, or adjust to your agenda. Because you already believe they belong. And show it.

We were made for belonging.

This new sense of self-worth is a stepping stone to establishing community. It's comfortable to eventually come to place where I am welcomed. As I am. With my strengths. And weaknesses. No need of pretending to be something I'm not.

CHAPTER FOUR

No pretense.

No performance.

My dear friend, David Richardson, taught me this principle even before I knew it's value. David was a ten-year-old who didn't fit in no matter what he tried. His home life was horrendous. Born with fetal alcohol syndrome, David had some serious issues. He was deemed extremely ADHD (Attention Deficit Hyperactivity Disorder), along with a host of other classifications. And he didn't have a dad. Even the man listed on his birth certificate wasn't legit.

Our church had started a tutoring program in conjunction with the local elementary school one fall, and the principal called to speak to me about David. "Tim, he's a handful. I really would like to see you work with him personally. It will be a challenge."

Really? How hard could it be to control one fifth

grade kid? I agreed. And then all hell broke lose.

Keeping David on task was impossible. His mouth was either running or he was. I learned in the first few minutes that he hated everything. His mom. Life. School. God. Even me.

And everyone hated David. So he thought. But at the end of day, I could understand why that might actually be true. This kid was a pain in the butt. But I liked him. A lot. He became mine. I wouldn't give up on the 10-year-old.

If there was going to be any progress made, he had to believe that I really liked him. Did I fake it? No. Something about him intrigued and irritating me.

But he was lovable.

As I was spending more time with David, I was still planning events for youth. Every week, I would invite him to come to church, youth group, retreats. Whatever was happening. No luck. I realized it didn't matter what the program entailed, David didn't care. It wasn't relevant to his world. Regardless of how cutting-edge it was in youth ministry, it didn't meet the needs of a kid with the tendency to cut.

So instead of continuing to beg him to come, I just stopped asking. Started entering his world more and more. As I did, something changed. David realized I believed in him just like he was. There was no expectation for change. And he didn't put on a mask with me. No games. I chose to believe in David even when boys from my church picked on him. Beat him up after school. And then I really took his side.

Like Jesus would have done.

But David's teen life was hard. More than once I spent days with him on suicide watch. Even holidays.

Together in a mental institution. Or jail. There he sat. Shoes. No shoelaces. Pants falling down. No belt.

He held his mom at knife-point one day while police held guns on him. I only hoped they didn't shoot him. He had so much potential to be a good kid.

When he got kicked-out of school or let go from jail, Cindy or I would pick him up on the road. "Need a ride, David?" "No. I don't want to be a bother to anyone." It was a common conversation between us.

He lived with my family for a while after his guardians had to ask him to leave their home. And then we had to kick him out of ours, too.

Tough love is tough.

Many, many times I held him in my arms and listened to him sob. "I want to love Jesus, Tim. I know he loves me. But I just don't know how to love."

CHAPTER FOUR

Over nine years I believed in David. Gave him my time. He knew his place with me. He was safe. Belonged. I watch him grow-up and eventually baptized him into Jesus Christ. A sincere commitment.

Then I buried him.

At age 19.

Thrown from the passenger seat of a car in a careless accident. Senseless. But in the course of his teenage life, he taught me the importance of giving young people a place to belong because the world won't accept you unless you try to fit in. Even the church world more than we like to admit. And youth groups.

David introduced me to countless teens just like him. Young people who only wanted a place to belong, too, without pretending to have it all together all the time. Or at all.

I'll tell David thank you for those lessons. Someday. Standing with Jesus. And we'll eat french fries again.

When we believe in young people as they are in Jesus' name, they have a better chance of believing in Jesus, too. They are drawn to a deity who loves them unconditionally. A principle the world doesn't tend to offer or understand. How much easier it is follow a faith whose source accepts me and gives me a place to belong in a community called the church.

BECOME

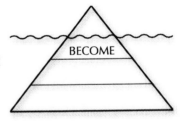

What things are you best at doing in life?

We all do many things adequately. Some even well. But everything is not our forté or expertise. Take golfing for example. I adore the game. Everything about it excites me. The life lessons it teaches. The beauty of a manicured

CHAPTER FOUR

course. The friendships made in a foursome on a sunny afternoon or rainy morning.

For years, I coached golf at the high school level. I passed on my love for the links. Taught fundamentals. Shared secrets. And showed teenage boys some ways to win their match.

Am I a great golfer? Better than a few. Maybe. But nothing spectacular at all. Average even on my best days on the green.

I didn't become a coach to play golf. Actually, my game got worse the more years I spent instructing. It wasn't my job to hone my swing but to help young men with theirs. While I watched and corrected their mistakes, I ran out of time to go out and play.

But I didn't mind so much.

Day after day at the driving range, I watched boys get

better. We started with 8 irons. And hit hundreds of them. For hours. Nothing else. No other club.

"Learn to hit an 8-iron, and you can hit anything." That was my mantra. They didn't like it at first.

"But I just got this new driver, coach."

"Great. I can't wait to see you grow into it and hit it a mile. Put it back in your bag. Get out your 8-iron."

I wasn't best at golfing. Coaching was more my deal. At the end of every season, I had one goal. Just one. To see each of my boys golf better than when they showed up the first day of practice.

And all play better than me someday.

It was easy not to care about my own game, as I saw each of theirs improve. And they learned to appreciate my love for the 8-iron, when their overall game got better from perfecting their swing by using it.

I was a decent golf coach with a simple philosophy:

1. I **believed** in their potential. Saw beneath the surface and recognized what could be.

2. I gave them a place to **belong**. Didn't care about their experience or equipment.

3. I provided opportunities for them to **become**. They learned to golf by golfing.

Can you imagine an athletic coaching inviting kids to come to the gym, the field, or the court only to sit and watch the adult mentor play the game? Exercise their gifts? Show off?

If my sons had to sit on a bench and cheer as the basketball coach taught them shooting, dribbling, and passing techniques but never gave them the ball, they'd walk away. And I would let them.

Becoming best at something is a matter practice. You actually get to do drills and get dirty. You may start small. Hit hundreds of 8-irons. But eventually you get in the game. Use every club in your bag.

You're not a spectator. Or member of the gallery.

Jesus was a coach. He recruited a team. A rag-tag bunch of boys no one else ever took into account. He believed in them. Gave them a chance to belong. And let them learn to become. Through experience.

Watch closely. You see them doing ministry. It wasn't long before he sent them out in pairs to run plays themselves.

They failed.

So he huddled them up. Gave a pep talk. Sent them

back into the game. Review the story for yourself in the sixth chapter of Mark.

Ever notice whose idea it was to feed the hungry crowd in Matthew 14? It wasn't Jesus who first mentioned the need. The disciples came to him. And he coached them. Every step of the way.

"Jesus, we should dismiss the people to get dinner."

"That's an awesome idea, but I don't think so."

Instead of running the ball or kicking the winning goal himself, Jesus called a different play.

"It was your idea, boys. You feed 'em."

"Seriously, Jesus? With what?"

"What do you have? Take an inventory."

The disciples came back with a sack lunch they

swiped off an elementary kid. "Hey, we found a Happy Meal. Here you go, Lord."

Now, this is the point in the story when Jesus really does something amazing. Everyone teaches that he blessed the sack lunch, but that doesn't begin to explain his next step. It is far greater. Much more intriguing and strategic.

He did bless something, but it wasn't a sandwich. No. He blessed the ingenuity and compassion of young people who recognized hungry people and human condition. The lunch box became secondary.

"Great idea, Phillip. I can get behind that idea for sure. Happy to help. Let me pray."

Jesus didn't say, "Watch how far I can hit this ball with my new driver, guys."

He coached. Gave others a chance to learn. Instructed. Corrected. Taught as needed. Didn't show off while others sat on the bench and watched.

And there were even leftovers.

Believing gives birth to belonging, which gives way to becoming what God intended his children to be.

When young people feel you believe in them, they gain greater confidence in who they are already. As confidence grows, a sense of belonging takes shape. In no time at all, the courage to step out and try something new evolves. Through trial, error, and your support in a healthy and safe environment, teens discover what they're good at, too.

They become.

In John 14:12, Jesus told his disciples they would do even greater things than they witnessed him doing.

And he made his statement reality by giving them all access to his power after he got out of the way. Upon his ascension (John 14:26 NIV).

The B-Praymid™ might best be understood in light of Luke 5:1-11. Jesus shows up on the scene and says to the professional fishermen, "Hey, let's go fishing."

An ignorant statement for sure from an amateur angler. There was a reason Peter and his pals were mending their nets in the middle of the day.

Because you don't fish at noon.

At night, fish school. In the shallows. On the surface. Where they are easiest to catch. Anyone with common sense understood how it worked. This is the way it had been done for years. Passed down for generations. Scripture doesn't say it, but you can bet it crossed their mind. "What is this guy talking about? We've never done it that way before!"

Now, I like to fish and when we fish for salmon on Lake Michigan, we occasionally use a technique called chumming. You take fish eggs, or spawn, and you throw handfuls of it out into the water. Basically, we feed the fish. Give them a little appetizer until they find the main course. My hook.

Practically, that's how these guys fished, too. Find a large crowd of fish feeding at night and snatch a few off the top with a net. No reason to work any harder than that really. It works.

Then after a long evening adrift, they would kick back under the afternoon sun, fix their gear, and get ready for the next big event.

In this story, Jesus basically says, "Ok, I know how you've done it in the past, but I'm going to show you a better way. Get ready. It won't make sense at first, but trust me, fellas."

CHANGE OF PLAN

As a teen, I thought I would be a high school running back. Speed, agility, and fearless. But my coach had a different idea. Harvey DeGood was great at recognizing talent and putting players where they would find the greatest success. My sophomore summer, he put me in the weight room all working on building upper body strength. He combined my bench press power with my speed and changed my position.

Nose guard. All 154 pounds of me.

He put me on the defensive line with one directive, "Get in the backfield and do some damage, Eldred."

It worked, and I loved it. I was not being hit, but inflicting pain on others. Awesome. That's the only reason to play high school football.

Even though I liked my new assignment, coach wanted me to understand his reasoning. He called a play and put me on offense at half-back during a game we were winning by 30 or 40 points. No problem. I knew the play and was confident I could still run the ball. Three yards was all I needed for a first down.

I got killed!

Totally missed the hole I was supposed to hit. Hammered in the backfield. By the nose guard no less.

Because a good coach recognized my gifts, he changed the plan and helped me find my place on the team. A position I could play with excellence. And achieve success while becoming better weekly.

Jesus changed the plan, too. Placed greater emphasis on the efforts. Product and effect was minimized. All in order to teach his team how to achieve greater success, as they found out how their talents could best be used in his kingdom game.

EXERCISE

Where do you show up?

Take the time to make a list of all the events, activities, and places the young people you serve live, work, and play. Perhaps this will require a little research. It might mean gathering athletic schedules. Recital dates. Concert information. Employers.

If you care for youth who attend multiple school districts, check out their school web sites. They will certainly list the details.

Before you start, you might need to go back and look at the attendance sheet with all the names of your kids you created. Find something out about each of them. Every one. Learn their likes, hobbies, and hangouts. Then add their events to your calendar. Place their activities on your agenda.

When you're done aligning your personal schedule to their world, make a master calendar others can use.

DOWNLOAD WORKSHEETS AT 4HOURYOUTHMINISTRY.COM

ESCAPE

To move yourself from being the primary player on the team, you need to place kids in positions best suited for them. That's what a good coach does. Helps them succeed in the right place.

Make a new list. Create roles or positions that need filled. Based upon the talents of each young person, begin to assign them to a role uniquely suited for the way God has gifted them.

Every young person should know how and where they fit, as you begin to bring out the best they have to offer.

DOWNLOAD WORKSHEETS AT 4HOURYOUTHMINISTRY.COM

NOTES

After praying about the previous chapter, take a moment to write down ideas or convictions that God is communicating. Listen to his leading. Guard yourself. The enemy is going to lie to you.

_____
_____
_____
_____
_____
_____
_____
_____
_____
_____
_____
_____
_____
_____

CHAPTER FIVE

RECOMMITMENT TO YOUTH <u>IN</u> MINISTRY

Over the last few years, I have become a student of student ministries and movements. The last century intrigues me most. In particular, the last 50 years is what I find most fascinating.

About the mid-1960's, the words 'youth ministry' became part of the Christian vernacular. Before that time, youth work was described with words like young people's societies, student unions, training unions. The title defined what youth were busy doing. With the new nomenclature also came a new definition of youth work, a new position in the church, even a new profession. The contemporary youth pastor was born. Paid youth ministry emerged on the scene in force.

Take an honest look. Notice as professional youth ministry has increased, youth <u>in</u> ministry has decreased. Youth doing the work of ministry.

A few decades ago, youth groups were actually led by youth. Adults helped navigate. Not drive. And the majority of young people active in a youth program stayed in the church. Discovered their place. Owned their faith. And remained involved leadership.

My good friend, Paul Fleishmann, President and Cofounder of the National Network of Youth Ministry (NNYM) said it this way in the fall 2008 issue of the

CHAPTER FIVE

Network Magazine in his commentary titled, Hands-Free Youth Ministry.

"Several of us "old timers" were talking recently about the alarming statistics of kids leaving the church – and their faith – after high school graduation. Despite the debate about which statistics to embrace, we all agreed that far too many do not seem to have a deeply-rooted commitment to Christ.

As we speculated about what is really going on, we reminisced about our teenage years and what it was like in our youth groups. Most of us were integrally involved. Some actually led the meetings and, at times, spoke in front of the group – even the whole church.

I was the leader of my Christian club, which met on campus after school. We had an "advisor," but it was pretty much up to us to plan and conduct the activities. Our weekly meeting was attended by 50 or more students, and we saw kids come to Christ and go into ministry.

The "aha moment" as we reminisced was the realization that our common denominator back then was our active involvement in ministry. Some were put on the spot and asked to serve. Sometimes we were trained; other times we had to "sink or swim." But in the process, we discovered our abilities and spiritual gifts. We experienced a hunger to know more and sharpen our skills. We developed an attitude of wanting to hear from the Lord and see Him work. We knew we were not adequate in ourselves.

In each case, someone believed in us enough to "entrust" the ministry to us. They took the risk that what we produced might not be to the level of what they could produce as adults. But the trade off was that we came to "own" the ministry. We cared about what happened. And we saw God use us in the lives of others.

He concludes.

Hands-free youth ministry doesn't mean we drop the baton. It just means that we entrust leadership to others – even as others first entrusted us.

As adults with good intentions stepped in to take over what young people had been doing just fine on their own for many years, teens intrinsically realized their gifts, talents, and abilities were no longer needed. Someone else would take care of making ministry happen. And youth were basically benched in the church.

Youth ministry became a spectator sport. Coaches would now take center court as young people were expected to sit, watch, and pretend they enjoyed seeing others play what used to be their position. Adults would plan the program. Put on a show.

Not a comfortable assessment to hear for us. Hard not to be a little defensive. Maybe even makes a few of us mad. And youth pastors cringe a little.

But don't take my word for it. Let's review the stats.

NUMBERS DON'T LIE

The recent studies that show youth leaving the church and their faith shortly after high school are no secret, as Paul Fleischmann eluded. They have been scrutinized and analyzed for a few years. Accepted by most as common sense. Dismissed by a few who prefer to remain blind.

Let's be honest. We have never spent more time, money, energy, on attracting youth and have less to show for our efforts. How do we explain it? How come swinging the bat harder and more often isn't getting the job done? After all, we're professionals.

Perhaps we need remedial swing training.

Believing in who we are as children of the Most High God has been an uphill battle from the beginning of time. Since Eden. We shouldn't be surprised to understand how the enemy's tactics have increased.

CHAPTER FIVE

From the garden until now, he's still on the prowl. Licking his lips. Looking to eat our lunch.

But he no longer has to be sneaky about his plan. Doesn't need to present fruit to entice his prey.

He has us polishing programs.

Admitting our current condition might be easier by looking back at how our predecessors handled the problem they faced with young people.

About 130 years ago, the church was dealing with the same issue. It wasn't sticky. Youth weren't staying. Despite the pretty programs of their time, congregations were losing their kids and kids were losing touch with their faith. Much like now.

One of the primary influences for paradigm shift then that has since become known as the forerunner to and father of modern youth ministry was the

Christian Endeavor movement. It began on a cold winter night in February, 1881, in Portland, Maine. A young pastor named, Dr. Francis E. Clark did something many leaders then, and today, are afraid to attempt. He raised the bar. Increased expectations.

On that evening, nearly 60 teens committed themselves to a new standard of teenage faith. It included a pledge to live daily for Jesus Christ. They also agreed to adhere to a few foundational principles to keep them grounded in their faith for a lifetime.

Dr. Clark was convicted that young people could make the same level of commitment to Jesus Christ as adults. And he made a covenant with youth. He promised to never do anything for young people in the church they could learn to do themselves.

In the end, the teens submitted to Jesus' authority and put their adolescent faith in action. They met

CHAPTER FIVE

weekly. Prayed, taught, planned, and responded to God's leading in their lives. Adults supported them from the backseat while youth found their place in the church and learned to lead by doing.

From a few dozen to a few million in a couple of decades they grew. All because one pastor expected more. Dared to go deeper. And got out of the way.

The movement flourished for decades until a few adults determined they could do it better. Slowly but surely, youth were no longer the leaders or the ones doing ministry in many churches. And the proverbial pendulum swung. Too far. In the wrong direction. Youth ministry replaced youth <u>in</u> ministry.

The new default is for adult youth pastors or volunteer youth workers to act more like program directors and less like spiritual mentors. And inadvertently, we have become addicts. By accident, of course.

The same issue of apathy they overcame at the turn of the twentieth century has come full circle to plague us now. Once again, we are trying to reach young people with artificial means of ministry when they are clearly asking for something simple

Something authentic. Relationships.

NOT A NEW PROBLEM

There was a time when the deception introduced by the enemy became so bad, God had to show up in person. He had been silent for a few hundred years up until then. Faith became a matter of performance and playacting. Religion dressed up in robes took center stage. And most were caught up in the act. Temples and techniques were both on the rise. Professionals ran the show. But God was about to reveal himself to the world. A mystery would soon be unveiled.

Jesus came.

A new definition of success was about to be written.

Instead of stepping in and making a big mess by bringing a new model of ministry to market, he did something uncommon even by today's Christian industry standards. He recruited the inexperienced, uneducated, and overlooked. He chose young men as an integral part of his plan.

The new teacher didn't set up shop. Start a new kind of rabbinical school. Run advertisements. Hire a band. Or print T-shirts. And unlike the high priests of his day, Jesus didn't wait for students to come to him. He went out and chose them.

HAND-PICKED PUPILS

Jesus calls us to completely unconventional methods. But he doesn't ask us to do something he didn't first demonstrate at the start of his own ministry.

Rabbi Jesus' ministry was risky. From day one, he required a level of faith and commitment most couldn't fathom accepting.

"Follow me. I take you to places you've never been. And teach you to fish in a new way. For people."

Nothing comfortable about that call. But before he invited them on the adventure, he introduced a new means of measuring.

Emphasis was placed on efforts. Unfamiliar to these seasoned seamen. Never considered by many. Ludicrous and laughable to most others.

Fishing in the middle of the day.

A new process trumped the old protocol. And the product would outweigh anything these fishermen ever witnessed before. But it worked. Almost sank the boat.

Jesus broke the rules. Establish new precedence. Began with a simple illustration we need to follow.

Forget most of what you know. And go deeper.

Down deep, where people cannot see or even begin to understand lie problems, needs, longings. Real-life issues. They are seldom recognized let alone given the attention they require because many refuse to dive to those depths with others.

Getting to a level of intimacy in lives that creates trust and openness requires time. Because I'm not going to let you see beyond my surface. Become transparent. Not until you earn the right. In time.

If you want to see who I am, what I feel, why I behave this way, wade beyond the shallows with me.

Take a chance. Risk relationship.

That's the cry of the generation we serve today.

And it's global.

It was the cry of the young people who followed Jesus, too. They were ready for a change. For revolution. The world was out of control. Their world. They dreamed of something better.

Desired significance.

Jesus delivered. By breaking religious rules. Blowing the minds of those who ran the show. And started a youth group.

Crazy plan.

Look closely. Read the gospels again. Research for yourself. See if you don't discover 11 or the 12 under the age of 20. Find another disciple besides Peter old enough to pay the temple tax (Matthew 17).

Jesus committed to change the world with wet-behind-the-ears-teens.

And from the first moment, he raised the bar. "Drop everything. Follow me." He taught them who they were. Showed them how to recognize the needs of others. Let them draw on his power. Gave them a safe place to land when they blew it. Instilled within them a sense of mission. Offered them a job. Gave them a chance, moved over, and made room.

He invested in pupils. He didn't invent programs.

Jesus committed to change the world with youth. We must recommit to his mode of operation.

But we can't go deeper until we let go.

Jesus' model and methods still work in our culture. Every culture. Because youth are the same today. As a matter of fact, in all my travels across the globe, I see little differences in young people. Race, ethnicity, demographic, denomination, even religion. Young people have a common need.

They want to matter.

Created in the image of our heavenly father, we all share crucial characteristics. Even before we know Jesus Christ or accept his atoning blood, God's DNA runs through our veins. Jeremiah 29:12 is true for all. He has a plan to give us hope and a future. Use us for his glory (Ephesians 1:11-12).

But it requires that someone teach us to recognize who we are as his children. Help us hear his voice. Say yes to his son.

Teens can make the same level of commitment to

Christ as adults. Jesus demonstrated it. History proves it. Dr. Clark knew it. One of the most famous stories of the Old Testament demonstrates the point.

THE BOY DAVID

In the seventeenth chapter of 2 Samuel, we find a fascinating story. But like much of scripture, we read over key insights pertinent to our predicament.

This account shows the people of God paralyzed. Now, we're not talking average, everyday citizens. But seasoned soldiers. Warriors. Armed. And ready.

Yet frozen. In fear.

God's chosen nation was faced with a giant dilemma named Goliath. A real threat. Insurmountable. Unbeatable. At least with their tactics and weapons.

And they weren't alone. The King, Senior Pastor,

Saul, was in the same boat. No idea what to do next. Desperate.

Then God sends a boy to do a man's job.

David, a mere kid, shows up to support his older brothers. And he walks into a camp of youth pastors of sorts. Just barges into their network meeting. Uninvited. These are trained leaders who have thrown everything in their arsenal at the problem they faced. All the youth ministry models, methods, tools, and resources at their disposal. But useless at this moment in the battle.

Verses 1-37 paints a clear picture of the event. Tells us how David was finally considered for the suicide mission. But only after he offered. He testified about God's goodness in his life. Claimed that he was called. Gifted. Equipped. Tired of sitting on the bench, watching from the sidelines.

CHAPTER FIVE

So he is taken to the head coach who says, "You're clearly not big enough to play nose guard. But we're getting killed out there. Suit up."

Read it for yourself.

"Then Saul dressed David in his own tunic. He put a coat of armor on him and a bronze helmet on his head. David fastened on his sword over the tunic and tried walking around, because he was not used to them. "I cannot go in these," he said to Saul, "because I am not used to them." So he took them off. Then he took his staff in his hand, chose five smooth stones from the stream, put them in the pouch of his shepherd's bag and, with his sling in his hand, approached the Philistine."

—1 Samuel 17:38-40 (NIV)

The king was in a pinch. Needed a kamikaze pilot or two on the front line to stop the run. David was volunteering. But Saul wanted to give him a fair chance (or just protect his own hide). So he loaded him down with his experience, expertise, education. Outfitted him in layers of the outdated.

And David declined. "Thank you, but no thanks. That won't work for my generation. It might have been cool in the 70's, 80's, 90's or ever the first ten years of this millennium, but I'll take my chances. If you don't mind, I prefer to depend on my dad. He's the Most High King, king. I have everything I need as his beloved. Because he taught me to recognize problems, respond with the skills he provided, and draw upon his power. Remember my resume?"

The process and power David knew Jesus passed on to his own youth group. And it has been preserved for you and me. God is raising up a generation to take their place in the battle, but we must slide aside.

Make room. God's commitment to use young people for his glory must now be our recommitment.

EXERCISE

Pastor Don Needham gave me the chance to sing my first solo. I was seven. Been singing ever since. Writing music. Leading worship. Pastor Jim Graham included me on his summer camp staff. Seventeen. Junior counselor. Three years later, assistant director.

Do you remember your first times? Maybe you taught a class. Planned an event. Spoke a message. Led a rally. Fought for a cause near to your heart. Might have succeed. Or failed.

Write down the item, the person's name who gave you permission, and the impact it had on your life. Then ask this question. Am I doing that for young people, too?

ITEM	NAME	IMPACT
_____	_____	_____
_____	_____	_____
_____	_____	_____
_____	_____	_____

DOWNLOAD WORKSHEETS AT 4HOURYOUTHMINISTRY.COM

ESCAPE

Following God's plan and escaping from any issue that has entrapped us is humanly impossible. It is only possible through prayer. Please take time to write down your heartbeat. Ask God to help you break free. To use your time more in align with his plan. Pray that he changes your mind-set. Your model will follow.

_____

_____

_____

_____

_____

_____

_____

_____

_____

_____

_____

NOTES

After praying about the previous chapter, take a moment to write down ideas or convictions that God is communicating. Listen to his leading. Guard yourself. The enemy is going to lie to you.

_____
_____
_____
_____
_____
_____
_____
_____
_____
_____
_____
_____

CHAPTER SIX

RECONFIGURING YOUR ROLE

Settling for less than God's best for my life has never been an option. He has called me to impact young people for Christ. And at my core, that is my passion.

I bet that describes you, too. You're not willing to settle for less either.

But I did. For a very long time.

Jesus came and showed us how to make disciples. There was nothing complicated about his methods. He spent time building relationships with young people. Instructed them as needed. Prepared them. Put them to work. Gave them just enough information to be dangerous. But that's when he is at his best. When we need him most (2 Corinthians 12:9-10).

Half prepared and half scared is how he left them at his ascension to heaven. But with a promise.

"I'm always with you. You can rely on my power."

Like you, I was brought up during a season in the church that appears to equate ministry to meeting. A quick look at where we spend our resources tells the truth. And we can't ignore it.

Eventually, my frustration with the lack of lasting results in young lives brought me to my knees.

God spoke. And I quit.

There were many moments that brought me to that point, but the following event was very profound. It really helped me understand why 'youth ministry' wasn't my calling after all.

ALONE SUCKS

A couple of years after the tragedy in Columbine High School when two young men turned a campus into a war zone, I was asked to monitor the students at our local high school who were doing a play on school violence called, "Bang, Bang, You're Dead."

My role was to spend time in classrooms engaging kids in conversations about the reason for and prevention of rising acts of violence in schools.

A few months before, I was meeting with my friend and youth ministry veteran, Rich Van Pelt. He had been involved in counseling for students in Littleton, Colorado. As people around the table probed Rich for insight that day, he left us with one word to explain the cause of the catastrophe from his educated perspective.

Alone.

He suggested that Eric and Dylan, the young gunmen, even together as a team of sorts, were still alone without accountability. It made sense to me.

During my time at our high school that day, I reflected on that piece of wisdom from Rich as a tool to challenge my captive audience. In every classroom I entered, I wrote one solitary word on the board in big block letters.

ALONE

"Can anyone tell me about that word?"

Silence. So I waited.

[You know if you actually ask kids serious questions they will give serious answers. The key is to shut up long enough for them to think through it, gain some courage, and speak up. That means treating them like young adults – not youngsters. More on that later.]

My goal that day was to create a level of empathy within the student body and staff. I wanted them to see themselves in each other, feel each other's insecurities, gain some understanding of their peers and pupils.

It was during the last class of the day when God showed up on the front row. He put on the flesh of a young man classified as Special Ed. And he proceeded to blow my mind.

The teen's name and face escape me, but I remember the his words like it was yesterday. They contained the greatest theology lesson I've ever heard. Genesis 2:18 for the twenty-first century was about to be spoken by a young man most of his classmates disregarded. God would share a message I needed to desperately hear. One that would effect the rest of my life, and hopefully, millions of other lives over time. Including yours.

I could sense the answer and see the tears both welling up in his eyes. No one interrupted, laughed, or remarked when he replied to the question none had yet answered. I directed my attention at him.

"Can you tell me about alone? Do you have something you'd like to share?"

I had clearly struck a nerve. It was as if the answer was festering inside for a lifetime. Like pricking a balloon filled with shaving cream. He exploded.

"Alone sucks!"

I finally knew my job right then and there.

Remove aloneness.

Shame on me for actually thinking any meeting I could ever plan would appeal to the level of pain and despair communicated in those two words. God clearly made this boy the mouthpiece to speak on behalf of generations of the helpless and harassed Jesus described for us in Matthew 9:36.

Just like my program couldn't attract David Richardson, it wasn't going to appeal to this boy either.

And that's the instant I knew I didn't want to do youth ministry as I understood it anymore.

I quit the full-time youth pastor thing. Fired myself. No more managing parents and programs. No more coming up with crazy ideas. Maybe I could even act my age and stop pretending it didn't hurt to wrestle kids 10 years younger than me on the youth room floor each week.

My new job description would be mentor, coach, and a friend of youth (like Jesus in John 15:15).

I would begin to do ministry with youth. Not do it for them anymore. It would become their program. Their ministry child. And begin with questions.

Ministry would be birthed from there.

IT STARTS WITH CONCEPTION

When my wife gave birth to our two sons, those were the greatest days of my life. For one simple reason. Because I was part of the conception process. It would have been a whole different story if Cindy would have delivered children I didn't help create.

As sons of daughters of the Most High God, the

youth we serve are created in his image. They have his heart. And more than anything, they want to know they are valued for who they are.

The easiest way to express that worth is to simply spend time with them. Get to know them. Earn their trust. And ask the right questions.

That's really what Jesus did with his first few.

In essence, he asked, "Do you want to change the world?" And a movement began as they followed. They eventually believed over time, but not before he gave them a chance to discover who they were.

They learned by doing and ended up following him for a lifetime. Because he went deeper. Saw beyond the surface. Wasn't afraid of letting them fail.

His plan worked. It was the perfect model. Easy. Authentic. Relational. Take time with teens.

CHAPTER SIX

You have to begin seeing yourself differently. If you want youth to learn to love Jesus and follow him, they must find a person in you and a place in the church where it is absolutely fine to soar or fall flat.

But they can't take ownership of their faith or their ministry without a chance to help conceive.

Here's is my favorite inquiry of kids. I ask three questions and take time for them to know I'm listening. These questions put everyone in their right role:

1. What breaks your heart lately?

2. If nothing was standing in your way, what would you do about that issue?

3. How can I help you?

With that simple inquisition, I just made their problem my priority. Instead of being both parts of the conception equation, I simply fertilize what God has already placed on their heart. And then I adopt what they conceive in prayer. And help nurture.

I no longer have to plan events. Or create activities to attract. Instead, I listen to their heart. Bring out the best in them. And help them employ their gifts and abilities to accomplish their God-inspired goals.

Their passion becomes the program. And they lead it.

It's easy for them to invite friends to come see the child they conceived and carried to full-term. Along the way, I provide counsel, support, encouragement.

When they don't know what to do, I don't give answers. I ask strategic questions. And they learn. Sometimes they trip and hit the ground. But I'm there to pick them up. Wipe 'em off. Send 'em out again.

And by the way, I don't beg. No pleading to attend

my program anymore. No need. They want to come to a ministry they own. It's common sense.

As youth in ministry, they learn how to listen to God and realize he has a plan for them. Today. Right now. They are a crucial part of his kingdom plan.

When I relinquished ownership of young people's ministry, I reconfigured my role. Instead of being the star on center stage, I determined to play a different part. Wear a different hat.

Stage manager. Director. Or sometimes producer. But always behind the scenes. Making sure the real cast of characters have what they need. Never putting myself in a position to upstage them. Ensuring their success. Encouraging their efforts. Emphasizing how Jesus is the one who blesses their obedience and accomplishes more than they can imagine.

I'm not a quarterback (or a nose guard anymore).

A coach. Helping call plays or even calling crucial time outs. But not running, passing, kicking, or even wiping off the game ball.

My new role is essentially what Paul meant in Ephesians 4:12, "Prepare saints for the work of service." Not prepare services for saints.

In 1987, Dr. Bob Laurent, wrote a book called, Keeping Your Teen in Touch with God. He listed the top ten reasons young people walked away from the church even then. And number one hasn't changed.

A lack of significant involvement.

Young people want to do more than show up and fill seats for an event you or I planned. And they definitely don't want to set the bench and watch adults dribble up and down the court or even dunk the ball in a dramatic fashion with cool lights and sounds.

When given the opportunity and support, young people can do everything youth pastors have been doing for way too long.

Make no mistake, you are desperately needed. But for a completely different role today. Mentor.

Below the waterline builds relationships, which become living examples of God's work in young people. As you mentor youth to do ministry, they will rise to the occasion. Rise above the crowd. And rise above expectations. As Christ gives them strength.

People will point to their efforts and marvel at what God is doing through them. They'll even overlook the missteps and mistakes youth make. Most of the time, you won't even be noticed. People will be too busy praising God for how he's working in young lives to care whether or not you're keeping office hours or not.

But as stage manger, there's only so much of you to go around. Burnout is bound to happen.

You have to increase your capacity. Build a team. Surround yourself and youth with more people who now see their role as the support system for teens.

They dream. You support.

A BOY NAMED SAMUEL

The account recorded in 1 Samuel 3 of a young boy named Samuel really intrigues me. It is relevant for today and for our purposes of recruiting adults to help. We see from the beginning of the story a young man ministering before the Lord under the support and tutelage of Eli. An experienced man of God. Youth and a youth pastor. Young person and a priest.

One night, Samuel awoke and heard someone call his name. Since no one else was around, he went to his mentor and spiritual leader, Eli, assuming is must be him who called.

"No. Please go back to bed, Samuel. I was in the middle of a good dream."

Again, he heard his name called.

And again went to Eli. Same response. "Son, go to bed. I need some sleep, and you're not helping me."

But when it happened a third time, Eli realized what was taking place. He instructed Samuel. "Next time you hear the voice call your name, say "Speak Lord. I'm listening."

Samuel had been serving the Lord in the temple. The youth pastor had been giving support, but things were about to change. And in the middle of the night, Eli understood his role. The mantle would be passed. He would help a young man recognize and respond to God's call on his life no matter the cost. Even if it meant his very job (and it did).

That's the heartbeat you will be prayerfully seeking for yourself and for those adults who will serve with you to mentor and guide this generation.

We are surrounded by young people God is calling to take their place in the cause of his son, Jesus. Young people he will use for his purpose to fulfill The Great Commission. But they don't know God's voice, yet. It's hard for them to discern God from gods in the midst a post modern world where truth is relative and spirituality takes many forms.

You need peers who are men and women of prayer. People of the Word. Determined not to be the star player anymore. But open to moving over. Teaching young people through example in personal relationships how to recognize God's voice in this noisy world. And how to respond as he calls them to step forward today.

It is not a difficult task, but it might sound awkward. Even odd to some with a modern youth ministry background. Youth lead. Adults support. A different approach for many today.

Just yesterday, I was in a conversation with a teller at my bank. I don't really know her well. Her husband is a family friend. My assumption is they are active in their church. And involved with youth.

The lobby was empty. So she felt comfortable asking, "Do you ever take your kids on retreats?"

Now, I never give an easy or short answer. My wife says it's because I like an audience. I prefer to believe that short answers shortcut real explanation and understanding (but Cindy's probably right).

I jumped into a conversation.

"No. Not unless they plan it, ask for it, or decide it's something they want to attend." I went on to explain that the meetings, events, activities, everything that takes place in our youth ministry is conceived, carried out, and birthed by the young people. "If not, we just don't do it."

She looked at me like I was from Mars (might be your reaction as well after 168 pages).

"Youth ministry is a means to an end. We produce leadership through discipleship, which takes place in relationships. Young people discover through doing."

I continued. "We see the possible and cultivate it. They create. We support their ministry." That was enough to make curious.

Her reply still has me perplexed. "Interesting. I have

never heard of a group like that. Sounds strange."

I was sad.

What could I do to help her understand how close she is to answering her calling as an adult youth leader? Yet, so far way from understanding her real role with youth.

Your job is not to do ministry, but help young people discover theirs, and we cannot accomplish that without helping them see their gifts, employ their talents, and learn as they take risks.

The role I now play in youth ministry, as we call it, is different than it was 20 years ago, and probably different than your job description, too.

While I do consider myself a full-time youth pastor, I don't get paid for it anymore. And I never spend more than 4 hours a week helping youth recognize and respond to God's call on their life.

No. Our church doesn't have paid youth ministry staff. But we do have a thriving youth program. Completely owned and operated by teens. It's not a huge group. Average in size. Just like our congregation.

There's 5 or 6 adult leaders just like me (but younger). We all coach a team of teens. Every team has a student captain who is responsible to make sure their mission-critical tasks are accomplished every week, month, quarter, and year.

We mentor. Disciple. And ask important questions.

Every adult takes no more than 4 hours to encourage, guide, instruct, and even correct team captains and group members as needed each week.

And we keep the Connect check boxes full.

CHAPTER SIX

We call. Text. Email. Stop by. Pick 'em up. Take them out. Meet face-to-face. And we lovingly hold them accountable for their mission and for their faith.

But we don't do their ministry for them.

It's hard for people to believe youth-led ministry when you describe it, so pastors have even flown in just to check it out. And left astonished. Because of God's grace and power working through youth.

Could I do ministry better than young people do? No. I do have a lot more experience, but it's not about creating a polished program. It's about helping youth become what God intended them to be.

Remember, youth ministry has inadvertently become about meetings. Discipleship has always been about process. And we must learn to value effort more than effect. Process more than product.

EXERCISE

Can you create a relationship with every young person in your church or corner of the world? No. Don't try. Your congregation or faith community is full of adults who would say yes to a 4-Hour Youth Ministry. But definitely not a full-time one.

The reason 20% of people in pews do 80% of the work is because there are no more senseless jobs to perform. Tasks that seem pointless. Nothing significant with real meaning. You're about to change that fact.

Find a handful of men and women just like you. Passionate for Jesus. Solid in their faith. And in love with teens. You're going to teach them everything you just read. More people will have a significant, personal ministry with a kid's name on it. Their number one qualification begins with this statement:

I believe young people can make the same level of commitment to Jesus Christ as adults; therefore, I promise to never do anything for young people they can learn to do themselves.

ESCAPE

Letter of Resignation

From the very beginning of this book, I asked you to quit your job. But that is your responsibility. And you'll have to explain why and define your new job description in your own words.

You can get started now. Create an outline. Make some notes. When you get ready to write the real thing and submit it to your church leadership, please send me copy. You can post in online at 4houryouthministry.com for others to read, too.

_____

_____

_____

_____

_____

_____

_____

_____

NOTES

After praying about the previous chapter, take a moment to write down ideas or convictions that God is communicating. Listen to his leading. Guard yourself. The enemy is going to lie to you.

_____

_____

_____

_____

_____

_____

_____

_____

_____

_____

_____

_____

_____

CONCLUSION

When you go below the waterline in young lives, you see what they're really made of and who God has created them to be. At least a glimpse of his glory revealed in their lives. As you see their potential and realize just how big their hearts are and what brilliant minds they have, you understand why it's not a big deal to give up *your* program for them to create one of their very own.

Abandoning full-time youth ministry to become a mentor of mentors who empower young people in just a few hours a week is where you will discover fulfillment of your real calling. But make no mistake, it's a hard habit to break.

As I said. I'm recovering. Not recovered. Still have a tendency to relapse if not careful. Even 17 years later.

But everything you hoped to eventually see take place in young lives will begin to happen before your eyes. And all you have to do is get out of the way and follow Jesus' example of discipleship. When you and your adult team believe in young people enough to give them a chance, they'll recognize your true commitment to their generation. It will be a shock, because more than likely, they've never seen such a thing in the church before.

And as you ask key questions of them, and really care enough to listen to their answers, they'll give you their heart. Their trust will follow. Please don't disappoint them by taking over what you just relinquished. Or you'll remove their sense of the belonging they were meant to always know in this life through faith in Jesus.

These new growing, confident, and courageous young people will astonish and amaze you with their talents, minds, compassion, and resilience. Given the chance to dream big dreams, try new things, and learn to prayerfully seek God and apply his Word to their lives and new found ministry, he will use their efforts for his glory. And very few will turn away or walk away from the church or their faith.

And then the extraordinary hard part comes. The hardest part of all in this whole 4-hour challenge.

You let go again. And again.

You send them off into the world to make disciples of Jesus, too. Just like he did after only a little more than three and a half years. But don't worry. He'll be there for them. And I bet you will be, too. The process never stops. A never-ending incubator of youth in ministry. The B-Pyramid™ repeats itself.

Believe builds relationships that **rally** youth and **encourages** them to live authentic lives. **Belong** gives them a place to find **resources** and **equips** them to take risks. **Become** is where they are **released** and **empowered** to be used by God. All resulting in transformed lives as God intended them to **be**.

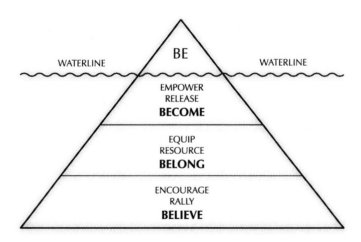

In the end, you find polished young lives, mature, and beautiful in Christ. They'll own their faith and ministry, as God receives the glory. And we let go.

MY FINAL WORDS

Even though this book gives you some principles to follow and practices to implement, it really isn't a youth ministry model. Not an easy paint-by-number approach. Or a three-step miracle cure. We have enough of those short-lived and shallow remedies.

This method of youth ministry is all about ***a change of mind***. A change of heart. Real change.

I have been asked to write out specifically how I do youth ministry in 4-hours a week like a playbook per se. But I can't give you a cut and dried formula to follow. That's why I shared my story, heart, and mind. Because you can't bypass relationship and discipleship with an accelerated program. That's been our mode of operation, and it has failed. My hope is that I have challenged your thinking and presented a biblical point of view that encourages your calling.

And while I may use the word 'I' throughout this book, God alone gets the glory. Nothing in this manuscript is new nor mine. Just a reminder of what he gave us in his precious Word when he told us that we are created for his purpose, even from the beginning of time. He humbles me to be a voice for this generation.

What does Jesus need from us to accomplish his plan in young people. To trust him. God still uses young people, and the Holy Spirit is still at work in their lives and in their world when we follow his plan.

Care about the right things.

Equip saints for the work of service. Help others be successful in their ministry.

APPENDIX

There is a model that supports the premise contained in 4-Hour Youth Ministry. It is time-tested, proven, global, and free of charge.

The last pages of this book explain the ministry of Christian Endeavor International and the Endeavor Movement, which is the structure and strategy churches across the world have used to produce youth in ministry who take action for Jesus Christ since 1881. God is still using this ministry.

CHRISTIAN ENDEAVOR EXPLAINED

WHAT MAKES ENDEAVOR DIFFERENT

The world would like youth to believe that they aren't as capable of service to Jesus Christ as adults are. That they can't be trusted to run their own ministry or make any significant, lasting impact on the world. That anything they create will lack depth.

A lot of young people believe the propaganda. It's your job to help youth prove the world wrong.

It won't be easy. Young people will need some convincing in order to begin to believe in their potential. That convincing may come in stages, as their small risks produce small victories, which fuel larger risks. One very important ingredient in the recipe for youth-set-free is your willingness to believe in their God-given potential.

Endeavor offers simple, significant steps that can lead youth to commit right now to living daily for Jesus Christ and taking hands-on action to make a difference in their world.

Many adults respond to this idea by shaking their heads. Such responsibility for such inexperienced individuals? Well, consider this: Throughout much of Bible history, average life expectancy was 20-30 years. The average life span in the Western world didn't reach 35 until the 1700s. In the year 1900, life expectancy in the United States was 47. Now it's in the high 70s.

We've become accustomed to viewing the first twenty years of life as an extended childhood. But for many of the people who lived the Bible's stories, the first twenty years…was life! Birth to grave. And when you expect, say, 50 percent fewer years on earth, each year becomes 100 percent more precious.

Throughout most of the world and most of human history, the adolescent and teen years were a time of responsibility and productivity. We, secluded on our island of history and geography, are the unusual ones.

So we ask, have the capabilities of young people changed just because we live longer today? No. A fourteen-year-old today has as much potential as a fourteen-year-old who grew up with Moses or David or Peter—maybe even more, given the education and technological resources available today.

These realities underlie the Christian Endeavor model. Among youth programs, Endeavor is unique in two important ways:

ENDEAVOR IS YOUTH-LED

It is Endeavor's position that youth learn to accept responsibility for their own faith—and for the faith of others—as they lead their own ministry with adult mentors acting as coaches. Young people run the show, participating in teams that are responsible for the various aspects of the Endeavor group.

What is more, Endeavor meets a critically important need in youth—the need to live up to their potential. Endeavor awakens in youth a passion for Jesus Christ and gives them the ability to do something significant today—not "some day." Youth emerge as leaders, and adults step aside, acting as mentors instead of program directors.

WHAT DOES AN ENDEAVOR GROUP LOOK LIKE?

An Endeavor group is comprised of young people from 12-21, who meet weekly and who plan and implement monthly service projects that meet needs in their community. These young people will organize themselves into teams and lead all aspects of the Endeavor group. A key group of young people act as a Leadership Team, and this team serves to direct the Endeavor group, allocate and organize the group's assets, and keep the group focused on its goals and spiritual development. Young people teach the weekly lessons, organize the monthly service projects, care for one another both during and outside of the weekly meetings, and communicate all important information about the Endeavor group's activities. Young people are prompted to set goals, make plans, and assess their progress during the weekly meetings—all guided by the weekly meeting model Endeavor provides. While young people strive for the strongest impact possible, adults mentor them, offering counsel and advice when needed and holding young people accountable to the goals they've set.

WHAT ADULTS WILL BE NEEDED TO HELP WITH ENDEAVOR?

Identify one Endeavor Mentor (likely the adult who reads this document first and who has functioned in the past as the youth leader or youth pastor). The Endeavor Mentor will recruit Team Mentors to guide the youth-led structure and provide support and care to the young people as they build and run their ministry. These Team Mentors may attend most or all weekly meetings and monthly service projects, assisting therein. Finally, Endeavor's discipleship program, Endeavor21, partners each young person in the Endeavor group with an adult Discipleship Mentor; these adults will work in a one-on-one context with young people to help them discover and develop their spiritual gifts and goals.

HOW WILL I LEARN TO CREATE AND BUILD AN ENDEAVOR?

Christian Endeavor provides seven Launch Workshops (including this one) to guide you through the processes of selecting key youth as leaders and launching the Endeavor group. The workshops include information to read, tips on understanding and applying the philosophical points of the Endeavor ministry model, and tools that assist mentors in moving from theory to reality. Each workshop will prompt the mentor and key student leaders to carry out certain action steps before moving on to the next workshop.

WHAT HAPPENS AT THE WEEKLY ENDEAVOR MEETING?

Endeavor has developed a four-week meeting cycle that includes community building, sharing, team participation (planning and preparation), service project planning and assessment, and Bible study and application. The weekly meeting curriculum is complete and user-friendly enough for even beginning Endeavorers to lead; it's also flexible enough for young people to adapt to their unique group. Each month, youth will identify an important need within their community and then plan and implement a service project to confront that need, assessing the successes and shortcomings after project completion. The curriculum also focuses on one Bible story each month, asking students to dive deeply into learning that story, consider it from all angles, and apply its lessons to real-life circumstances. Weekly Bible activities challenge Endeavorers to take action and apply life-skills and spiritual virtues in their daily lives. In later meetings, young people have a chance to share the ways they met these challenges. We encourage you to look at the weekly meeting guides to learn more about how the weekly meetings support young people as they take control of their ministry.

WHAT ARE THE FIRST STEPS IN CREATING OUR ENDEAVOR?

First, commit to the core principles of Endeavor and determine to allow young people to reach their full potential by letting them take the reins. Next, commit to reading and understanding the information included in the workshops, then use the tools that Endeavor provides to build your Endeavor group. Finally and most significantly, pray for God's direction and guidance as you begin the hard work of finding the right people to propel this vision forward. Youth-led ministry works. This is proven. But it will take the commitment of your faith community's leadership, young people, and adult mentors to make it work. Specifically, begin praying for God's wisdom in choosing and recruiting mentors as your right-hand men and women. Also, you will need to quickly identify and bring on-board at least two or three key youth who also will progress with you through these workshops, and help you achieve buy-in from the congregation and the youth group at large.

WHAT SUPPORT AND MATERIALS WILL BE PROVIDED?

Youth-led ministry may seem daunting, and it will

take work, but making the switch can be easier and quicker than you might guess. Endeavor offers a plan and tools for converting your ministry, including workshops for getting church and youth buy-in, setting up a discipleship program, and organizing your Endeavor's teams, leadership, and mentors. Plus, we want to support you personally as you begin this exciting journey. Endeavor staff-members are available to talk, help brainstorm, and pray with as you make the switch. This doesn't happen overnight, so to assist your group in your journey, Endeavor provides a year's worth of weekly meeting materials, intended to be youth-led.

Endeavor materials are provided free to members of the movement. You can register in moments and download resources immediately. When you see the impact of Endeavor on your faith community, prayerfully consider a yearly financial pledge, because the Endeavor movement is member-supported.

STARTING AN ENDEAVOR

Endeavor exists to give every young person a chance to serve Jesus Christ and find their places in His cause by the age of 21.

The mission is accomplished when young people are challenged and supported by adult mentors to:

- Make A Commitment
- Build A Foundation
- Take Action

The commitment begins with a promise.

ENDEAVOR PLEDGE FOR YOUTH

Trusting Jesus Christ for strength, I promise to **pray** to him every day, to **study** God's Word, to **serve** others, to **share** my faith, and to endeavor to **live** a Christian life.

ENDEAVOR PLEDGE FOR ADULTS

Believing young people can make the same commitment to Jesus Christ as adults, I promise to challenge young people to the highest level of service and dedication.

With God's help, I promise:

- To teach by example the principles of Christian Endeavor

- To support the mission and ministry of Christian youth

- To equip youth to lead their peers in the cause of Jesus Christ

- To involve youth in the life and the work of the church

- To recognize and celebrate their achievements

BUILD A FOUNDATION

A foundation is built as young people practice the principles of Endeavor highlighted in the pledge. Youth meet weekly to apply these five principles, develop their talents, and discover their roles within their Endeavor group.

Principles of Endeavor

- Pray: Connect with God as we discover our significance in His plan.

- Study: Let God's Word equip us as we prepare to serve others.

- Serve: Respect one another as, together, we give ourselves away in Christ's cause.

- Share: Practice accountability as we share God's love with the world.

- Live: Take risks and fail forward as we follow Jesus' leading in our lives.

TAKE ACTION

Endeavor groups respond to needs in their community. Young people work on teams to accomplish tasks critical to their mission. As attendance grows, teams increase and take responsibility for all aspects of operating the Endeavor group.

The details of starting an Endeavor group are covered in all the free materials from Christian Endeavor. They provide all the practical resources you need to begin your 4-Hour Youth Ministry.

Register for free today at endeavormovement.com or contact them at 800.260.3234 in the USA.

ABOUT THE AUTHOR

Timothy Eldred currently serves as the Executive Director of Christian Endeavor International. He continues to serve in pastoral leadership in the local church. When he is not travel, Tim spends his life in Michigan with his wife, Cindy, their two sons.

Tim's personal mission is to be a mouthpiece God can use to deliver this generation from the bondage of low expectations.

timothyeldred.com
facebook.com/timothyeldred
Twitter @timothyeldred